GODZ CREATIVE ZONE

HOW THE KINGDOM OF GOD WORKS

LADY JANICE

authorHOUSE®

AuthorHouse™
1663 Liberty Drive
Bloomington, IN 47403
www.authorhouse.com
Phone: 833-262-8899

Published by AuthorHouse 04/27/2021

ISBN: 978-1-6655-2352-3 (sc)
ISBN: 978-1-6655-2351-6 (e)

DEDICATION

TO MY LOVELY RIGHTEOUS MOTHER AND FATHER,
TO ALL MY MENTORS AND ONE SPECIAL MAN OF GOD
WHO OPENED MY EYES TO THE TRUTH OF GODS
WORD. TO MY FAMILY WHO GAVE ME THE INSPIRATION
AND TIME TO SEND THESE LETTERS OUT TO THE
BELOVED BODY OF CHRIST OF WHICH I AM A PART OF.
THESE BOOKS ARE HERE FOR YOUR EDIFICATION AND
INSTRUCTION ON HOW TO LIVE IN A DUAL KINGDOM.
ONE ON EARTH AND THE KINGDOM OF GOD THAT HAS
COME. HOLY GHOST IS IN CHARGE THRU JESUS NAME.

MAY GOD, THE CREATOR OF ALL, GET ALL THE GLORY

CONTENTS

PART I

PART II

PART I

CHAPTER ONE

WYSIWYG TRUE STORY

" The power to change, the power to be... it's all a matter of what you really see."

THE LADY SPEAKS

For what you see is what you get, the 'WYSIWYG Principle" in THE CREATIVE GOD ZONE. If you are reading this book, you have become a part of my dream. For as long as I can remember, I have dreamed of having the ability to help people change virtually anything in their life.

I love people, and that love has spurred me on a quest for answers to life and How to make it work. For life was meant to work; that was the design. I want to help mankind. The whole world needs a good dose of hope... and a dream, and I learned How to dream, and I learned How to believe my dream.

Many were the times that adverse situations, unfriendly circumstances, and negative people and things came into my life to rob me of my dreams. The opportunities were numerous for me to quit believing my dream, but each time adversity of any kind hit me, I had a choice to make, keep believing in my dreams, or stop and accept status -quo - to either let this be my tombstone or make it my steppingstone. I chose to make it my steppingstone. Each obstacle would cause me to become even more determined in my own heart that no one nor anything would stop or deter me from realizing my dreams. GOD gave me those dreams, and they are mine, and I will relinquish them to no one!!!

See, anyone can dream, but you must believe your dream, and that dream will sustain you. In the place between dreaming the dream and realizing that dream is a place called living. Of which we all know too well.

Life is USER Friendly when you learn the keys of the kingdom and how to apply GOD'S WORD when you gain access. We are in a race in our Christian walk; we are all running to win. We are not in a thirty-yard dash but rather like a long-distance race in which you must gain endurance.

Of the many things involved in developing endurance, these are four particularly important.

DETERMINATION: YOU MUST BE DETERMINED.

DISCIPLINE: YOU MUST LEARN DISCIPLINE OF LIFE.

DARING: YOU MUST BE DARING ENOUGH TO DO WHATEVER IT TAKES TO WIN.

DESPERATION: YOU MUST WANT YOUR DREAM WITH GREAT DESPERATION.

I must dream with endurance, for to that one that endures, to the end will get a Crown of Life.

Life is glorious!!! Life is to be loved and lived with excitement, enthusiasm, and zest. Living, really living, has become a lifestyle for me. It is great. I live life on purpose. The wonderment of life and making it work for me has attracted many people to me. Those people seek me out with all their problems and dilemmas. They even call me their "counselor."

They are seeking to tap into a reservoir of knowledge that I have learned. They watch me closely, applying wisdom to that knowledge, and see the profit of GOD'S WORD. I am talking about all those who consider themselves average or less but want to change. AND YOU MUST REALLY DESIRE CHANGE BEFORE IT WILL COME.

You say, "I have tried to change in the past with no actual results." Yes, I know many folks who, because of past efforts of trying to change by willpower alone to make changes in their life, failed miserably in that mission. What happened was they gave mental assent to what they had read or were told, and it did not work for them. What they needed was an internalization of that truth. The mind's eye needed to be enlightened.

You must be able to change what you see with your mind's eye to affect real change. When that happens, you will be able to take charge of your life immediately and control your thought process and become a focused people with concentrated effort, a people with a dream realized, ENTERING THE CREATIVE GOD ZONE.

Now I know because of our society and longstanding assumptions that we have accepted as truths for our lives. We believe that it must take a long time for us to make significant changes—the reality of this matter that it is not so. The real reason it seems so difficult to affect the change we need is that most of us do not know How to change. We want to. The desire for change is there, but we do not know How to achieve it.

I have learned some secrets or mysteries of the ages. They are all found in the BIBLE, which I will call our "instruction manual." I based these principles on GOD'S WORD and backed up totally by HIS Authority. When applied as instructed, they bring life.

"My son, (child) give attention to my words, incline your ears to my sayings. Do not let them depart from your eyes. Keep them in the midst of your heart. For they are life to those, who find them and health to all their flesh. Keep your heart with all diligence, for out of it spring the issues of life; put away from you a deceitful and negative mouth." (Proverbs 4:20-24)

I have learned how to unlock the power to create with the keys given in the instruction manual. I have learned what I see, really see in my mind's eye: I could have it. Just like our natural eyes develop problems with vision, so do our spirit's eyes.

Sometimes our mind's eye (vision) becomes hazy, unfocused. I found that when that would happen, things quit working in my life ...it was at a standstill.

I have become frustrated over being on high center. I would rev my engine up (so to speak) but would not go anywhere. In my desperation, I would go back to what GOD said and take the keys in the instruction manual to access what I needed.

WOULD I USE THE KEY TO UNLOCK THE CREATIVITY TO PRODUCE IN MY LIFE THE CREATIVE GOD ZONE.

So, whenever I realized, for whatever reason, my vision in my mind's eye was fuzzy, or I was losing my sight, I would get my spirit eyes adjusted and again be on track and have those things I desired and see my dreams realized.

That sounds easy, but it is a very disciplined practice. You must be able to have your "The Mind's Eye ENLIGHTENED, TO GOD'S TRUTH." You must become focused and locked onto that dream and see that dream!!

To gain a better understanding of GOD'S WORD and how HIS KINGDOM operates, we will delve back into the original Hebrew language from which the Old Testament is written and into the original Greek language from which the New Testament was written.

These are very precise languages to give us the exact WORD so that we can break it down.

The instructions will be in an understandable lay term of information, to put it into practice in our life, as applied to concepts and principles to life skills that work.

We will look at many things that are facts in this world's scientific realm and apply the HIGHER TRUTH of GOD'S WORD to come to the correct conclusion and ability to make life work and work abundantly. We are in this world, but not of this world.

We hear much about the mind-body connection, which is a topic of discussion and debate among scientists, researchers, theologians, caregivers, and laymen alike. Much has been written and studied on the subject.

Clinicians have long observed there are meaningful mind-body interactions, and now with a "health savvy" public, things have had to change from scientists who have either been unwilling or unable to explain the scientific underpinnings of the mind-body connection.

We can be ever so thankful that psychology and sociology are catching up with the CREATOR OF ALL THINGS... with what HE said in HIS WORD all along.

With the advent of new tools for studying and measuring, and comprehending immunology, the long-ESTRANGED DISCIPLINES of behavior and medicines are finding common ground and catching up with the BIBLE.

Examples of some ways the mind affects the body:

COMMON COLD: More people are likely to get a cold when they are stressed or depressed. Only recently have studies dissected and discuss the emotional components that seem to put people most at risk.

It was reported by a psychologist at Carnegie Mellon University that previously, in research, the people who were intentionally exposed to measured doses of cold viruses, the research showed the psychological state before infection thus could predict whether a person would get sick. The higher the person scored on a test of stressful life events (such as having experienced a divorce, death of a spouse, etc.) current perceived stress-related issues. That gave UNABLE the sense to cope with current demands and negative emotional states such as depression -causes, which made a person more likely to catch a cold.

CANCER: Dr. David Spiegel of the University of California made headlines back in 1989 with a study showing patients with advanced breast cancer who participated in weekly group therapy sessions, reported those who participated SURVIVED NEARLY

Twice as LONG as patients who did not. Since then, other researchers have come to similar conclusions with melanoma, leukemia, lymphoma, etc.

Further studies are being conducted to see whether that survival difference may be due to IMMUNOLOGICAL OR HORMONAL CHANGES that resulted from the counseling group session. These findings may NOT be made public for many years, but a trial test is being done to test that theory.

Dr. Spiegel made a statement, 'We're not curing cancer here, but what we are doing is getting a handle on the factors that AFFECT DISEASE PROGRESSION, AND HOPEFULLY THAT MIGHT LEAD to an understanding of the mechanisms by which the mind can affect the body." The mind-body connection - no wonder we are told in GOD'S WORD not to be anxious - stressful for nothing.

AIDS: Psychologist Margaret E. Kemeny at the University of California has made an intensive study of men infected with HI\/ virus (AIDS) to see whether feelings of bereavement speed progression toward Full-Blown AIDS. .

In her findings, SHE HAS FOUND THE LOSS OF A LOVER, but not a friend, often accelerates immune-system failure, as shown by a decline in T-cell levels and other immune indicators.

CARE-GIVERS: A study done at Ohio State University has found that people with long-term CARE-GIVING Responsibilities, such as caring for an ailing spouse, are at risk of becoming clinically depressed and also have immune systems that don't respond well to standard challenges. You can really die of a broken heart.

A top doctor at Johns Hopkins University says, 'What's more, you can die of a voodoo curse." That is because your brain sends the HEART messages that can stop it from beating if you are terrified or suffering devastating emotional stress.

Studies have been done on both rats and humans to pinpoint the parts of the brain that LINKS the heart to thought and emotions. They have found a key to controlling the heart in an area of the brain called the INSULAR CORTEX. The insular cortex findings may be sensitive to stress, which results in increased HEART RATE per Neurology Department Cerebral Vascular Division at John Hopkins.

If the INSULAR CORTEX is damaged by an EXTREME EMOTIONAL STRESS, it can cause more than just an increased heart rate. It can cause sudden death. That is what most likely happens when people die suddenly for no apparent reason after losing a mate. The INSULAR CORTEX is also affected by fear, which IS why many people die after becoming the target of a voodoo curse.

Now, I know in AMERICA, if someone were to say to someone else, "I am going to place a spell on you," they would laugh you out of the door. But in cultures where people BELIEVE that spirits can be called on to do you harm, the threat of a voodoo curse goes right to the INSULAR CORTEX and can result in "instantaneous death."

We could go on with various examples of studies and research facts, but the idea that the mind might be a key player in health and disease is by no means new.

GOD'S WORD is filled with instructions about guarding and renewing our mind to HIS WORD -which is positive.

Physicians in ancient Greece believe the body and soul must be treated together. Sir William Osler, the Johns Hopkins physician, widely considered the father of modem medicine, once said that to predict the outcome of tuberculosis in a patient, "It's just as important to know what is going on in a man's head as it is in his chest." (Distributed by Los Angeles Times - Washington Post News Service.)

The book you are embracing and the journey you are embarking on is one of the greatest you will ever be a part of. GOD THE CREATOR created us in HIS image and designed us to work in our life; Spirit, SOUL, and BODY areas.

We have just NOT known these truths. From the beginning of all time, God put in HIS WORD - THE BIBLE - our instruction manual for life.

I am so sorry Clergy failed to teach people these GOD-GIVEN TRUTHS to help people live life and that more abundantly.

How do you see yourself? ▪ An ideal form exists within any block of stone. The sculptor's task is merely to release the perfection within. (Michelangelo Buonarotti 1475- 1564)

So... Let us begin-Take hold of my hands and let us begin our journey into the

"CREATIVE GOD ZONE."

CHAPTER TWO

ENDING BRINGS THE BEGINNING

Right now, you may be a person that had a dream and lost that dream. For whatever reason, someone or something took it from you. You may be at a place I have found myself often. I call this place "THE END OF THE ROAD." Where it looks as if you will never make it as if there is no way out. But do not feel bad for being there, just do not stay there!!!

In the WORD OF GOD, it clearly tells us, GOD will always make a way where there is no way if you will trust HIM to. "GOD IS A GOOD GOD." God only has good in mind for you. Sometimes the dark clouds roll in over our heads, and we cannot see. Our way gets dark and slippery, or our path is hidden from us.

We need our instruction Manual (GOD'S WORD, the BIBLE)) to be a lamp under our feet and a light unto our path. GOD has given us an instruction Manual which is a directive for our life, the BIBLE.

I will be using several examples of men who learned those secrets of the Ages. In this book, I will be using my evidence of their lives and how applying these same truths will cause you to succeed every time you enter the CREATIVE GOD ZONE in life that God has shown us in His Word.

Even in our day and time, some people have been using these scriptural principles and, in many cases, did not know it.

I do hope you are at your APEX of desperation, for only desperate men and women win. There are many books out in the marketplace which are excellent. To mention some, "Seeds of Greatness," "Awaken the Giant Within," and "In Search of Excellence." I could go on and on.

This book is written totally with the emphasis on instructions from the WORD OF GOD, and you must apply those instructions to make life work every time on purpose, in the CREATIVE GOD ZONE. This information is based totally on the WORD OF GOD, and it will transform your life if you choose to allow it. But you must make that conscious choice and do it.

JESUS has given us "Keys to the Kingdom." He has given us everything we need to live life and live it more abundantly now. Our problem, or the challenge, is - we do not know how to implement the instructions given us in the WORD OF GOD. We do not know what to do with the keys HE has given us.

It is like we have been given keys to a new Mercedes. Wouldn't that be great? We would be elated and excited. But unless we use the keys, we will never go anywhere. We will never drive that new Mercedes down the road. It would never work.

Just because you have the keys for the new car, that does not automatically start the vehicle and give you access to drive it. You must know what to do with those keys and use them. Keys give access. Keys unlock. Keys by themselves are of no value unless used appropriately. The keys presented in this book will provide you with access to life and the power to live that life abundantly.

Seek ye first how the Kingdom of God works, then all the things needed in life will be given.

It has been said by a dear friend of mine, Mary Banos, "There are people who never bloom, some people bloom only bloom once, but you bloom over and repeatedly." That is outstanding!

It has been asked repeatedly, 'What is your secret?"

Well, today is the day to share with the entire world that secret, that mystery of the Ages. Twill give detail by detail the keys that JESUS Himself gave. I will share with you how to use them so that you may gain access into a realm of life that you never thought possible. You will enter the CREATIVE GOD ZONE.

But you must choose to read carefully and be very attentive to the words and apply them in your life as principles or laws and allow them to become life skills for you as a winner.

Please remember, truth always is progressive, and it has three degrees or levels, ALWAYS.

The truth taught will be:

REVELATION
ILLUMINATION
INSPIRATION

Revelation is to find out new truth or find something revealed to you, you did not know before. Illumination is an understanding of what has been revealed to you. Inspiration is the carrying out of the truth revealed and illuminated.

You may think that many things happen to many people and things along the way in life. Choosing to live your life by your own choice is the greatest freedom you will ever have, for it is only when you exercise your right to decide that you can also exercise your right to change. If you would like to know your choices, look at yourself and the life you have lived so far. What you see are the choices you have made. CHOICES by S. Helmstetter.

GOD THE CREATOR has given us - mankind -the created, the power of choice, and HE will NOT take that away.

Today, as you read this book, you are all the sum total of your past decisions. Let today be the end of failing and the beginning of winning.

You, my friend, are the one who will choose to win, decide to change, decide to overcome, or you will be the one to say, "I cannot do it." You say, "But you just don't know my circumstances, you don't know the family I come from, and you don't know Where I live. Because if you did, you would not be telling me how this could work for me." GOD says I give you a choice today. Do you want life or death, blessing or curse? YOU CHOOSE!!!

I most assuredly am telling you it will work for you. There may be some things you will have to choose to unlearn and re-learn correctly and have the courage and boldness to do it. But I believe you can.

You are the reason I wrote this book. YOU CAN DO IT! I did it. YOU CAN!

This quote so aptly applies to me ... "I am one of those people who just can't help getting a kick out of life, even when it is a kick in the teeth." (Patty Adler, 1953)

"It does not matter How many lemons life seems to pass my way - I just make more lemonade." (THE LADY SPEAKS)

Life is the greatest gift!! Life is to be lived. Life, at times, maybe a struggle, but it is worth it. Life is a journey, an exciting adventure. Life is wonderful day by day. Life is to be lived and spent ever so wisely, for we cannot store it up. Life is to be lived NOW and enjoyed. "YOU MUST WANT SUCCESS BADLY."

In this world we live, you can find geniuses on any skid row by the same token, you can find average intellects as presidents of banks, but it is what pushes you from inside. (Quote by Charley Winner, 1976.)

LADY JANICE

What do you see? What pushes you on? What is your dream? For what you see, you will truly be. What you see is what you will get, is a principle in THE CREATIVE GOD ZONE.

MY WIFE AND MY MOTHER-IN-LAW
They are both in this picture — Find them

What do you see? Everyone at times need an EPHIPHANY!

CHAPTER THREE

WILL THE DREAM
COME FORWARD?

The greatest gift you can give someone is life. God has given us life-Life now, and life eternal through HIS SON, JESUS CHRIST.

Today, all the way back to the beginning of time, there are many examples of men and women who have had dreams and would not let that dream be taken away. Yet others have lost their dreams. It took someone or something to bring it forth in their life.

THAT IS THE VERY HEARTBEAT AND CRUX OF THIS BOOK-To give you hope, to stir up the gift of life GOD placed within you, to help you re-focus and once again, to have your eyes enlightened to GOD'S WORD of Truth, to see you dream, and to see your vision once more.

JESUS CHRIST went about doing good wherever he went. He gave hope to the hopeless. He called his disciples to be followers or imitators of HIM. He was our Prototype of what we were to be. Are you following Him?

In this book we are trying to meet that challenge. We live in a land of plenty here in America, but there is such a spirit of hopelessness. The reason for so much hopelessness is that people have lost vision, lost their way, their dream.

The Bible tells us a people without a vision or dream will perish. A vision - a dream. Which is the intent of this book. To inspire you to bring forth in your life once more. To have hope!

We may not know exactly what tomorrow holds, BUT WE KNOW WHO HOLDS TOMORROW. And that gives me confidence, gives me hope.

GOD does not want you to perish. GOD is a GOOD GOD and only wants good for you. IF YOU WANT A TOMORROW, THEN TOMORROW BEGINS TODAY. That is the way spiritual language works.

GOD tells us about tomorrow in your dreams and visions. He tells those to you today so you can make it tomorrow. GOD gives dreams. If you can see a thing in your mind's eye, you can have it.

There is a significant rise in the popularity of the psychic phenomenon all over the world. Reason being, people are scared, fearful, afraid to live, afraid to die. They want to live, but do not know how. These people will go to great lengths to know about tomorrow. They want to be soothed on the symptoms plaguing their life with despair, lack, poverty, and hopelessness. They just want to be told everything is going to be fine, even if it is a lie...

But what if we really meet the challenge of the hour and get down to ROOT CAUSES - Get down to the person's real self and begin to apply the instruction from the Manual, Gods Word.

Begin to bring forth the dream design, the blueprint GOD has for that person. Give them a sure WORD, a sure path or way to follow. That GOD is speaking especially to them about their tomorrow, and they begin to believe and do it. THEN YOU WILL HAVE HOPE, CONFIDENCE, YOU WILL MAKE IT TOMORROW AND YOU WILL LIVE TODAY.

This is exciting information. GOD gives you dreams - visions about tomorrow. But GOD is so wise, HE tells you today. HE does that so you can make it into tomorrow. There are so many adverse and negative factors present in our world today. IF you do not change the way you see things, you will eventually be overtaken by your circumstances and it might even kill you.

It is a powerful truth, in THE CREATIVE GOD ZONE, what you see is what you get, (WYSIWYG Principle.) We humans have been given the ability to create, either for positive or negative. We are all artists, and we are continually painting a picture of our future life onto the canvas of our heart.

Most Christians are continuously going through one crisis after another and are totally clueless as to why. With their Own mouth they continually paint bad, gloom-and doom pictures on the canvases of their heart.

The instruction manual clearly says, "Out of the abundance of the heart, a man speaks. Whatever a man thinketh in his heart, so is he." Far too many people do not realize the value of ordered conversation.

The BIBLE - INSTRUCTION MANUAL- says, "Let the weak say I am strong." GOD will supply all my needs according to HIS riches in glory by one CHRIST JESUS. So therefore, I will not lack. When you begin to think those things, that is what you will begin to be continually producing in your life.

GOD only has good things for you. HIS WORD says all good things come from the Father of Lights. GOD is a GOOD GOD; GOD is a caring and concerned GOD. HE did not create you to be a loser. You are made in HIS image, and GOD created you to be a winner, just like HIM. Losing is foreign to GOD.

You cannot continue to go around doing, living, and saying any old thing you want, living undisciplined, unfocused, and thinking you can open your mouth up one time or a few times and say, "GOD will supply my needs."

NO, HE WON'T! IF YOU HAVE NOT FOLLOWED HIS INSTRUCTION, THAT PROMISE IS NOT YOURS.

There is a process you must learn. You will have to have preparatory time. Spend time in THE WORD, meditating that WORD OF GOD. You must learn ORDERED CONVERSATION. You must develop something in your spirit. You need to become conscious of the words you speak. Make them words of blessing to your life, not a curse.

You paint pictures, images, precepts on your spirit and heart by words. Words are powerful containers of life. The instruction manual says by your words you will be justified or condemned. I am not talking just one day! But a lifestyle! We can be much compared to a silkworm. We are producing and spinning every day by our words.

Our words are so important. They will either protect us or bind us up.

WORDS ARE POWERFUL!

For example, many people will come to me for counseling and say, Minister, something is wrong. It is like suddenly; I find things not going right. What is wrong? Well, you can answer that very quickly if you just listen to their words the last two to three years.

YOU ARE THE SUM TOTAL OF WHAT YOU HAVE BEEN SAYING YOU ARE.

You are the result of your speaking for the last few years - right or wrong. You may be thinking that is not fair! Well, whether it is fair or not, it is a fact. You are living in the sum total of what you released from your mouth over the past few years.

Thought patterns over a period of years will internalize and create the things inside of us. If you are a fearful person, you can change that. With the (WYSISYG Principle) IN THE CREATIVE GOD ZONE.

In the INSTRUCTION MANUAL, Joshua 1:8, GOD told Joshua to meditate the WORD day and night. When you literally study that out, you will find HE is talking about.

The very first thing in the morning and the last thing at night. I have observed over the years YOUR MENTAL PATTERN for the day is established in the first ten minutes you are awake. What you focus your mind on for those first ten minutes will establish your thought patterns for the day.

Another interesting observation: You can establish a mental pattern somewhere between thirty and forty days. You can either break a mental pattern or habit or make one. Whatever you see is what you get. What you focus your mind on for long periods of time will eventually proceed to your spirit.

Once it gets into your spirit, it will start to come out of your mouth. Once it starts coming out of your mouth, you will have it. You will have it whether it be good or bad, negative, or positive in THE CREATIVE GOD ZONE.

I know we live in a society that bombards us day and night with negative inputs or trivial stuff to stimulate us to keep us unfocused. That is why it is so necessary to be WASHED BY THE WORD OF GOD. Renew your mind to the WORD OF GOD.

I know that sometimes that is hard to do with schedules and obligations. You are tired, worn-out, weak, depressed and the very last thing you want to do is come to GOD, get into the instruction manual, meditate HIS WORD (Bible) and pray.

Did you know in Psalm 23 of the INSTRUCTION MANUAL it says that if you will do just that, that the Shepherd, the LORD who is a good SHEPHERD, will restore our soul, WHICH IS OUR MIND, WILL, EMOTION, AND INTELLECT.

If you will let the WORD OF GOD speak to you, wash you, renew you, you will be lifted, encouraged. You will have life and love.

"I will boast of all HIS kindness to me. Let all who are discouraged take heart." (Psalm 34:2)

GOD desires good for you. He will lift you up. You may be as the Prodigal Son who had been out living a hard, fast life and ended up on skid row. HE decided HE had enough and needed to be restored. The Prodigal Son came back to his beginnings. His father came out and met him, made him feel welcome, encouraged him, lifted him up and restored him.

That is what GOD desires for you. If you will let GOD'S WORD get in your spirit, meditate it, speak it, start to live it, start to praise GOD for His mercy and goodness, you will find it will start to change the way you think and live.

"Rejoice the soul (mind, will emotion, intellect) of your servant. For to you, O' Lord, I will lift up my soul." (Psalm 86:4)

But you can change all of that. You just must choose to do that. Do not be like many people I have observed in the church. For reasons I am not sure of, these people have decided to be unteachable, stiff-necked, and will not learn any new truths. They wallow in all their old habits and refuse to change and wonder why life will not work.

Now, they may give MENTAL ASSENT to the WORD OF GOD. They know the WORD by memory, but NOT by the power to change their lives. They do not want to hear the progressive truth of GOD'S revered WORD and apply it to their life.

Mental assent means that we are agreeing the WORD is true, we just do not want to do it. You must leave the old ways and be renewed to GOD'S ways. Quit living by feelings, and line those feelings, line your life, your actions, all these must line up with the WORD OF GOD.

You need to make a conscious decision from this day forward to base everything you say or do totally on the WORD OF GOD. If you will hear and do what I am saying in this book, be like a wise man that considers all things and applies the WORD. Use the INSTRUCTION MANUAL.

Bring your faith to line up with what GOD'S WORD says and you will find your life will work like a fine-tuned jet.

You will have your dreams. You will not perish because your eyes will be opened to see what GOD sees. What you see is what you get (WYSIWYG Principle) in the CREATIVE GOD ZONE.

CHAPTER FOUR

GOD DOES NOT MAKE LOSERS

Did you know that being a loser is foreign to GOD, THE CREATOR? There is not one place in the scripture that you can find GOD even lost once. So why do we accept being losers in life? Losers at love, losers at health, losers at happiness, losers at relationships, losers at everything?

Why? Yes, we have been somewhat conditioned by external influence. But we need to change. It is totally against GOD'S nature to lose. GOD is our CREATOR and our HEAVENLY FATHER. Don't we get our nature from our parents?

Is it normal for a dog to bark? Yes. Then would not you say it was abnormal for puppies if they cannot bark? Is it normal for fish to swim? Yes. What fish had babies that would not swim? That would be abnormal. Does GOD always win? Then it is abnormal for HIS children to lose. It is totally out of character of a born-again Christian to lose at anything.

NOW, I KNOW THAT GOES AGAINST THE CROSS GRAIN OF OUR RELIGION AND OUR FEELINGS, BUT NONE THE LESS, IT IS TRUE.

Yes, we will have tribulations and trials and persecutions. GOD'S WORD tells us that. But it also says, "Thanks be to GOD, who leads us in triumph" over and over. CAN YOU CONCEIVE THIS TRUTH?

Your circumstances will come and go, but your vision-dream must not change. Your mouth confession for good must not change. We are instructed to hold fast to our profession of faith. Never let it go! Hold fast to your confession of faith.

In our instruction manual there are three-hundred and sixty-five scriptures that speak against fear. FEAR IS THE MOST DESTRUCTIVE FORCE ON THE PLANET. You cannot have. Faith and fear together. They are opposing forces. DO NOT FEAR. Do not let fear of any kind control you.

Be like Psalmist David, and see yourself go through your circumstances, your problems. Go beyond it. You were made in GOD'S image; GOD wins. What about you? Need to change your image - your behavior? We, children of GOD made in HIS Own image, need to consider this story.

When Alexander the Great ruled all the known world, he made.

it his policy to hear any appeal made to him. One day, they brought a young soldier before Alexander for trial. The young man wore the tunic of Alexander's army. 'With what is his charges?" asked Alexander, who held absolute Authority in all matters, and there would be no appeal of his verdict.

"He is charged with cowardice in battle," answered the prosecutor.

A great hush fell over the crowd gathered in the judgment hall. They knew Alexander, as a general, expected his men to be as gallant as he, since he, himself, did not push his soldiers, but led them into the thick of battle.

Alexander looked at the young soldier who was a mere youth, fair-haired and still too young to shave. The angry scowl on his face left and was replaced by an understanding smile. 'What is your name, soldier?" 'Worthy King," responded the youth. "My name is as yours, Alexander." Anger came back into Alexander's face and he leapt to his feet. Alexander grabbed the soldier's tunic. 'Young soldier," he spoke with impressive control. "Either change your name or change your behavior."

CHRISTIAN ARE YOU WORTHY OF HIS NAME? If not, change your behavior! For what you see is what you will get in the CREATATIVE GOD ZONE. You must quit acting and being a loser. Begin to see yourself as a winner. Overcome all adversity. Change your behavior by changing how you see yourself.

How do you see yourself? Like Gideon saw himself in the Old Testament, he was in a winepress, tramping grapes and running for his life - scared.

And an Angel of the Lord came to him and said, "OH, mighty man of valor." Gideon said, "Who, me? Not me. I am a chicken. I am scared. I am no man of valor."

GOD gave a dream of who and WHAT he would become. Gideon entered the CREATIVE GOD ZONE. GOD sees the end result and backs up to your beginning. Gideon's end result was, he was a mighty man of valor. But he had to change How he saw himself.

Peter was SIMON, which meant unstable as water and became Peter, meaning little rock. Simon was a wishy-washy loudmouth. But GOD saw his end result. Peter - a rock - PETER HAD TO CHANGE THE WAY HE SAW HIMSELF AND SO WILL YOU!

ISRAEL, WHO WAS JACOB, which meant liar, cheater, and supplanter, became ISRAEL. That means prince that has power with GOD. Jacob had to change the way he saw himself. He dreamed a dream.

Then there was Abraham the Father of the Faith.

Abram became Abraham, which means a father of a multitude.

These were all men who had to change the way they saw themselves and how things were. But they got a vision - dreams of victorious outcomes. GOD always determines your purpose first. GOD sets your course before you are ever born and works everything after the counsel of HIS will. And GOD will take every negative adverse situation that comes against you and will work it into the good plan and purpose for your life. You choose to let HIM...

THE BIBLE IS FULL OF NUMEROUS ACCOUNTS TO GIVE HOPE TO THE HOPELESS. When GOD gives the dreams and visions and shows you something about tomorrow, about you and your life, you can make it no matter what the circumstances.

But what is so unfortunate when you do not have a dream or vision of GOD'S next of events for you?

When you do not have the correct image that GOD has for you, then when disaster strikes; cancer, poverty, or whatever, to take your life, most people do not know.

How to handle it. Most people just give up and say, 'Well, this is my time to go."

LET ME ASK IS IT? Some will even try to fight with all they have to fight with, but to no avail. Most do not win. They lose. They die.

What most people fail to realize is most battles are not won when they get struck Down with a problem or in a no-win situation or the worst of all circumstances. That is not when they are won. But, regrettably, that is when they try to find out what tomorrow holds.

By asking, does GOD have a plan for my life? Am I going to see another day? Will I ever...and what they try to do is battle when the disaster strikes, and they usually lose the battle because they were unprepared - unarmed with no vision/dream - NO IMAGE OF THEIR "GLORIOUS END" RESULT TO SUSTAIN THEM.

GOD says, "My people perish for lack of knowledge of needing a dream and believing that dream and realizing that dream. You need a dream, a vision to sustain you." You must learn how to live and enter the CREATIVE GOD ZONE. I believe GOD has allowed this book to be written just for you!

When GOD spoke to Abraham, he told him, "I am going to make you a father of a multitude, which is a victorious outcome. GOD did NOT tell Abraham he would have problems in his home - problems with a king - must travel. But GOD GAVE HIM THE VICTORIOUS OUTCOME.

Even though Abraham had so many negative circumstances in his life, it did not matter. He remembered his vision/word of GOD. HE SAW THE IMAGE GOD GAVE HIM, and said, "I cannot die now. I cannot cease to exist." He had a dream, a destiny to complete, because GOD originally said to him what the future held.

And what I am trying to do is to get you from today into tomorrow.

And that is what I want you to see.

Satan and his wiles do not want you to inherit your promise of life and that more abundantly. Therefore, most of us stagger when someone comes and tells us this excellent report of the promises from GOD for life that we can have.

Do not stagger at HIS GOOD WORD. Keep reading, believing, and doing. YOUR LIFE IS GOING TO WORK!! I BELIEVE IN WHAT I AM SAYING TO YOU. I BELIEVE YOU WILL LIVE AND MAKE it NO MATTER WHAT.

The psychic phenomenon is getting so big all you have to do is turn on the television to see that. The reason is that no one knows about tomorrow. But I have splendid news. I KNOW SOMEONE WHO DOES!!

Job in the Old Testament made this statement in his despair. "My days are swifter than a weaver's shuttle. They come to an end without hope." In other words, if I do not have my hopes, they will come to an end very quickly. And IF you do not get hope, your life may end very quickly. If I lose hope, I have nothing to work towards. JESUS came to give hope!

JESUS IS THE HOPE OF THE WORLD!

I write this book to give you courage and hope, to live and live life to its fullest and to have your life work, NOW!

There are three vital ingredients we need to have fulfillment in life. ***FAITH***, ***HOPE*** and ***LOVE***. The greatest, the Bible says, is love. But right in the middle of faith and love is HOPE. Hope only comes to you when somebody says things are going to be well. Everything looks great. Things will and are working out fine. SOMETHING HAPPENS TO YOU, HAPPENS TO THE CHEMISTRY IN YOU. Something happens when you are told you are going to get an increase, be successful, your body is healthy, or are going to be.in shape. You are in excellent condition and will live another fifty years.

DID YOU KNOW THERE IS AN ADJUSTMENT IN YOUR MENTAL Attitude THAT CAUSES A CHANGE IN YOUR CHEMISTRY WHEN YOU HEAR SOMETHING ABOUT YOUR TOMORROW? Just like when you hear something bad. Someone says you will probably live another six months, and that is all they give you. Most people told that would probably live their six months out and die, even though it was not the disease that killed them. That is a fact.

Doctors, psychiatrists, some of whom are my dearest friends, they will confirm this to be true. MOST DIE OF MENTAL ANGUISH. Many people die millions of times in their mind and then die physically. Someone gave them a bad, disagreeable report of themselves.

My hope is in the LORD and in HIS WORD, I SHALL LIVE TO TELL THE GOOD NEWS, TO GIVE HOPE TO ANYONE THAT WILL HEAR...FOR AS LONG AS YOU ARE BREATHING, THERE IS HOPE. (Lady Janice)

Hope comes from *TIQUAH,* a Hebrew word meaning hope, expectation, something yearned for and anticipated eagerly. It is something for which one awaits to look in a particular direction. It is to stretch like a rope. *"For you are my hope, OH, LORD GOD" (Psalm 71:5)*

GOD is showing HIS desire to you. That desire is for blessing, blessing to take you from death into life. To transform, to change you from the valley of trouble and into the door of hope, which gives access to the CREATIVE GOD ZONE.

CHAPTER FIVE

OUR MIND IS A POWERFUL THING

Your mind has the power to heal, or it has the power to kill. Let me relate this true story that was written in the eighteen hundred during the French Revolution.

They wanted to do an experiment to see how effectively the mind could cure or kill by the way it was programmed. They took a prisoner who was condemned to death. They told him what they wanted to do. They told him they wanted to slit his wrist and see how long it would take him to bleed to death. So, every day for about a month, they would come in and tell him what they planned on doing.

They told him, 'We will split your wrist. You will feel the blood run down your wrist. You will start to feel woozy, and you will go to sleep and never wake up." They repeated this over and over. THEY WERE TELLING HIS EMOTIONS WHAT TO EXPECT. Finally came the big day. They took him to a room, laid him on a table, put a curtain between him and his wrist and said, "Okay. We must cut the wrist. You will begin to feel the blood run down and you will drift off to sleep, lapse into unconsciousness, and die." And he did.

But the only thing they did was run a sharp piece of ice across his wrist and put a liquid of the consistency of blood down his arm. HIS EMOTIONS

DID THE REST. HIS THOUGHT PRODUCED DEATH. They had programmed his emotions to go to sleep and die, and he did.

That is what has happened to us in the day and time in which we live. Constantly programmed to be sick, fall and be defeated.

"As a man thinketh in his heart, so is he." (Proverbs 23:7) This does not say as a man feels. It says as a man thinketh.

Thoughts - (Greek work, Dialogismos) - is the thinking of a man deliberating with himself. (self-talk, settling accounts, suspicious because of his state of indecision. inward reasoning, dialogue with oneself, questions, consideration, deliberation, turning over thoughts in the mind.)

What you think establishes the path for what your emotions and will, WILL FOLLOW! The only exception to that is when things are taken directly into your spirit.

That does not happen that often but does as times bypass the mind and emotions.

For example, when you are sitting and hearing the WORD OF GOD or when you are reading, or GOD is speaking directly to you, that goes directly to your spirit. It does not necessarily go through your mind or emotions but could. GOD can do whatever. Can come through a TRAUMATIC EXPERIENCE, whether good or bad, can bypass and go directly to your spirit. Have you ever felt something, and you KNEW it went immediately into your spirit? It literally bypassed the area of your soul.

We are all a three-part being. Spirit, SOUL, AND BODY. The Soulish Realm is the mind, will, emotion and intellect.

NOW, your mind is like a computer. IT does not generate thought. It only takes in the stimulus of what you hear, or taste, or any of your five senses. Then it goes through and is catalogued by your mind and your emotions respond to it. And then if there is an action that needs to take place, it either happens or does not happen.

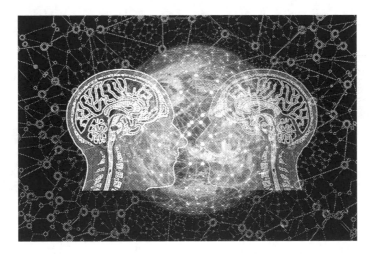

The way you are going to be directly results from the way you think... period. THE MIND IS POWERFUL! The mind is actually the battlefield for where the victory is, either won or lost. For you to overcome, you must have your spirit-man in charge, as a new creation, renewed.

You must learn the spiritual side of you and How it operates and get the spiritual man to override and influence your soulish realm. But you will have to do some things, as a matter of fact, a lot of things with your mind and your thought process. And I am talking about practical things.

The Scripture, "For though we walk in the flesh, we do not war according to the flesh." The flesh means your senses or emotions. We are not to walk by our emotions or feelings.

"For the weapons of our warfare are not carnal, but mighty in GOD for pulling Down strongholds, casting Down imaginations, arguments, and every high thing that exalts itself against the Knowledge of GOD, bringing EVERY THOUGHT into the captivity to the obedience of Christ. Being ready to punish all disobedience when your obedience is fulfilled." (II Corinthians 10:3-6)

The *word CASTING DOWN, in Greek, is KATHERSOSIS*, which means to destroy, dislodge, or to pull Down.

That means we are to do something. We must respond with action. GOD'S WORD demands a response, always. The Greek word for *logic is.*

LOGOSMAS, which means understanding, reasoning, logic.

The *Greek word for imagination is ANOIA*, which means our creative side of our mind.

DIA, in the Greek, simply means through. Through logic-through imagination.

Now, here in II Corinthians, he is talking metaphorically about something that is lifted up, exalted, or built up. He is talking about STRONGHOLDS And those strongholds, you will find, are PATTERNS/Habits that have been built into the way we think. (Thought patterns.)

Most people cannot exert any control over their thoughts. Their thoughts just run rampant, controlled by anyone or anything. We have many EXTERNAL CONTROLLING INFLUENCES over our minds and in our lives.

He says that these strongholds are built into our minds by constant repetition, which has caused us to act, react and to respond in a certain way. Strongholds are patterns or habits that we have built into the way we think. Have you ever heard someone say, "That person is just bent on doing that no matter what you say or do."? They are bent, or that is the way they are molded.

Several years back, we took a trip down the east coast. My husband and I went there for some rest and relaxation. As we walked the beaches, we found some trees that will grow to a certain height and then they bend over, level with the ground, and grow. They are quite unusual and uniquely beautiful. The reason is that the offshore winds are extraordinarily strong and as the young tree begins to grow, the winds are so constant; they blow the trees over. Instead of growing up, the wind's influence causes the trees to grow horizontal or parallel to the ground.

That is the way it is with an incredibly young person. They are easily molded. Whether we believe it, daily we are molding and impacting people's life, directly and indirectly. We are being molded.

My dad, Frank Evans, a minister of the Gospel for fifty years plus, was the wisest man that ever lived. (At least in my eyes.) He was the father of eleven children, with me being the tenth. When we all had our children, Dad always encouraged us to train up our children in the way they should go. And when they are old, they will not depart. He encouraged us to raise our children correctly under the admonition and nurture of the LORD. He said, INVEST THE TIME IN YOUR CHILDREN, FOR THE REWARDS ARE GREAT. He would say, "The way a little twig is bent, that is the way the tree will Grow. "My Dad was right. He was so wise. My three children are grown and How wonderful they turned out. My oldest daughter, Tammy, gave me a plaque which reads:

CHILDREN LEARN WHAT THEY LIVE
If children live with criticism, they learn to condemn.
If children live with hostility, they learn to fight.
If children live with ridicule, they learn to be shy.
If children live with shame, they learn to feel guilty.
If children live with tolerance, they learn to feel patience.
If children live with encouragement, they learn confidence.
If children live with praise, they learn to appreciate.
If children live with approval, they learn to like themselves.
*If children live with acceptance and friendship; they learn to find love in the
    world.*
-By Dorothy Lee Nolte

We are all influenced, whether positive or negative, from the way we are born. And now, I too encourage my children to love and raise their children correctly. As Dad taught, 'THE WAY A LITTLE TWIG IS BENT THAT IS THE WAY THE TREE WILL GROW.'

Now, for that tree on the beaches, it is too late for it to stand upright, because it has already been bent and molded. But for you, it is NOT too late.

Throughout the years, our world and society have been squeezing us, molding us, and to some extent, has been remarkably successful. But the BIBLE says you need to do something about that. We have allowed strongholds, thought patterns, to be built in our minds. Whether willingly or unwillingly, someone or something has been built in these strongholds, and they need to be removed.

You were not born that way. When you were born, you were born a baby - not one with a bad temper, not a pessimist or optimist, just a baby. That is all. Everything else is LEARNED RESPONSE.

Apostle Paul said, "I HAVE LEARNED TO BE CONTENT, NO MATTER WHAT STATE OR CIRCUMSTANCE I AM IN."

That is a learned response, and if you are not content, you can learn to be so. Contentment is not in the things you possess, whether great or small. Contentment is a state of mind and you can learn contentment.

You can teach yourself. Contentment is a state of mind that you can teach yourself. If you are not content, you can learn to be so.

Have you ever had a travel bug, or gypsy blood, or traveling fever? I have. In my younger days, I have always wanted to live there, live here, go there, go here. I love the islands, the oceans, the desert, the mountains, the plains, the cities, the country, the jungles... I love to travel. I love GOD'S big, wonderful earth, and all that is in it. Nothing is wrong with enjoying all of that and travel. But if it results from not being contented, you need to change that. But before I understood some things, I was never content. I was always wanting to be somewhere else, doing something else. I was never content. I was always Down the road somewhere else, never content.

Can you relate? Remember, this is about getting to the truth and being honest with yourself and with GOD so we can make the right choices in life, therefore causing life to work!

CONTENTMENT IS A LEARNED RESPONSE.

Then JESUS said to those Jews who believed Him, "If you abide in my WORD, you are my disciples indeed, and you shall know the truth and the truth shall make you free." (John 8:31-32)

Not set free - *MAKE FREE*. This is JESUS talking. It says the truth makes you free. Freedom is always associated with truth. Bondage or strongholds are always associated with lies or deception.

Listen, you may not remember exactly or memorize enough to quote scriptures when centering in on this information. Just remember, use Biblical concepts or principles as a lifestyle. For what you think is what determines what you do!

The enemy's strategy to destroy you is to use tools of deception. If he can keep you deceived, he can keep you in bondage or a stronghold. Let us address deception, his number one tool. The root of deception is from the enemy. JESUS' number one warning for last days is, "DO NOT BE DECEIVED."

Now, there are certain ways we are deceived to believe lies.

We will only address three.

FIRST could be just growing up in tradition. When growing up, you can establish some things in your life that may be what a parent, a teacher, or an authority figure told you, and it simply was NOT TRUE.

SECOND is what you determined to be true. This is through personal experiences. One way is manipulation. Most people that are manipulators have determined in their hearts that the only way they could get what they wanted was to manipulate. The only problem with manipulation is that it only works three to four times. But those folks determined in their heart that the only way they could get what they wanted was to become manipulators, to manipulate. So now, in their thought process. Their mind, they have determined that to be true, - it was a lie.

THE THIRD area is the lies of the enemy. Let me tell you How he talks to you. See if Satan says, "Janice, you are really stupid and you do not have any idea of

What you are doing. You are so stupid; you always make mistakes. You never do anything right. You are just one big screw-up."

If that happened, it would be easy for me to refute that because I would know where it was coming from. I would say, "No, that is not true!" But he is more subtle and crafty than that. He does not speak to you in an accusatory manner, but rather speaks to you in personal pronouns. He says, "I never do anything right. I can never get ahead. I always make stupid mistakes. I am not worthy. I am ugly. I am fat. I will never amount to anything. My life will always be a mess. I will never get out of this."

And by keeping you in that, you think you are generating that thought. You think that it is coming out of your spirit.

Remember, you do not generate thoughts out of your mind.

That is why we need to renew our thought process daily with the good, positive WORD OF GOD. So, the reasoning faculty of your mind says if your spirit is saying it to you, it must be true. But it is not. It is a lie of the enemy. The enemy also gets you with RAPID-FIRE THINKING.

And when you already have a problem with fear, worry and poor self-image, the enemy uses rapid-fire thinking as an amazingly effective tool.

The definition of *rapid-fire thinking* is when he gets you to think so many thoughts within just a matter of seconds to get you from point A to spiral Down to point B, the gutter!!

In the book of Psalms, it talks about *the noisome pestilence*. I believe that is an accurate description of *rapid-fire thinking*. And when you take that over into the extreme, it can produce manic depression. That is where you get manic depression. People who have rapid-fire thinking, they begin to run around the room and clean up and do all kinds of things.

Thoughts are powerful! Take, for example, a person relating a story about having a flat tire on the road. They said they got out, looked at the tire, and saw it was flat. And within a matter of minutes, they decided in their thoughts what their fate will be. They thought, "THEY HAVE A FLAT. THEY ARE STRANDED NOW AND WILL BE TAKEN AWAY BY SOMEONE DOWN A COUNTRY ROAD, ROBBED AND LEFT FOR DEAD. THEIR CHILDREN WILL GROW UP ORPHANS." AND ALL THAT WAS FROM A FLAT.

TIRE! By the time the police got there to aid, they were a blithering idiot all because of uncontrollable thoughts.

If you operate in fear, worry and anxiety, the enemy will shoot those thoughts so fast that you are overwhelmed before you can even decide. Fear is destructive.

You need to ask and answer: WHO IS. IN CONTROL OF YOUR THOUGHT PROCESS? The enemy will tell you, you are powerless over anything, powerless over your life. He will say you are powerless over your future, your past, and nothing will ever change for you because you have never been able to control anything.

So, what makes you think you can control it now?

He will tell you everything that controls your life is outside of yourself, that there is nothing you can do to change this, that your wife, husband, job, money, circumstances, environment, that everyone and everything run your life, that you have no control, no choice.

This is important for you to know. YOUR OBEDIENCE TO A PARTICULAR THING ESTABLISHES THAT AS AN AUTHORITY

IN YOUR LIFE. AND YOU CHOOSE THAT. If you are disobedient to continue in a situation or a particular habit, then you establish that as an authority in your life.

For example, a six-inch cigarette can control your life. I have heard people say that they are their Own man, do without a cigarette for two hours and become a wild man. The cigarette controls them.

By the same token, if you are obedient to the WORD OF GOD, you establish that as an authority. You establish what is authoritative in your life. If you are obedient to GOD'S WORD and prompting the spirit. That is the Authority. What does HE say and do? The BIBLE tells us we can pull Down imaginations and every high thing that exalts itself against the knowledge of GOD. These things contradict the WORD OF GOD.

For example, the BIBLE says HE gives us peace. But yet few people have peace or have experienced peace. We need to allow that to come upon us. Peace is one of the fruits of the spirit, and fruit must be developed. They are only received in seed form. It has got to be nurtured, grown, and matured. You can have a seed, but this does not mean you will have a crop. I may have watermelon seeds, but I do not have a crop out of them because I did not develop or plant the seeds.

HE says, "Casting Down arguments and every high thing that exalts itself against the Knowledge of GOD, bringing EVERY THOUGHT into captivity to the obedience of Christ. This is almost incomprehensible, mind-boggling to say the least. It says every thought. This verse is telling us we can have total control over our thinking process. Someone or something is going to have control over your thinking process.

If you do not take control of your mind, will, emotion, and intellect, there are many waiting in line, such as media, government, world...to control it, squeeze it, shove it, mold it, bend it until you think the way you want to think. That is what HE is talking about here.

You need to choose to focus, pay attention, to take control of your thinking process. You cannot control your mind for at least an hour without it drifting out the Window, so to speak, you are losing control and something else is taking control. Quit allowing your mind to become unfocused, to run wild, become subject to anything and everything, thoughts of sickness, poverty, lack, fear, death ... It does not matter How old or who you are. You need to start taking control of your thinking process. Today, start where you are. You must decide to bring every thought Down. It is a discipline that can be learned, and you can do it.

See, when l was a young girl, I read Nancy Drew mystery books. I would become so focused and intense; the house could disintegrate around me and I would never know it. My mother could talk to me and I could not even hear her. I was totally engrossed, out of this world. I was focused.

I believe and am suggesting to you that this is what you need to do. Lock on - focus on the WORD OF GOD. You ask, "HOW can I when I cannot even concentrate for five minutes?"

One reason it is so hard for the people of our day and time to concentrate these days is because we have been educated and programmed over the last few years to expect a SCENE CHANGE OR NEW EXTERNA.L STIMULUS every couple of seconds by television and other media. Many have become addicted to this kind of bombardment. The possibility that television and other stimulus of our modem world has insidiously removed the ability for us to concentrate.

Because of this, I advocate that when people read, meditate, or hear teaching, they cannot help not being able to concentrate, because they crave an image change. That is the way they have been programmed.

CASE STUDY: At one of the leading universities, an English professor was reported doing a study on the CONCENTRATION CRISIS among people in general. The test was a man was seated in front of television with a videocassette recorder. They played a video of a 1950 show, JACK BENNY. The subject was asked to count how long it was before there was a scene/image change. He counted 1001, 1002, 1003, 1004. Every time he reached 1004 there was a scene change. This exercise lasted five minutes, then went on to the next test.

A video from the sixties was played, THE FUGITIVE. He repeated the instructions of counting the seconds between each interval of image change. It was noticeably less than the show of the fifties.

A video of the seventies, KUNG FU. The intervals between scene change were about three seconds, a reduction of about one second in twenty years.

In a video from the eighties show, MIAMI VICE, the intervals were changing so fast it was too difficult to keep up with. Everyone and one-half to two seconds were a scene change. Every two seconds or less, a visual change.

Consider the stimulus of the nineties. Can you see why it is so difficult for people to concentrate or focus these days? Now here 2021 look at the people and your own life.

Next time you turn on the television, try this experiment during just a commercial. Because of our environment and the way, we are being silently programmed; it is removing the ability for us to concentrate or control our thought process. Instead of you overseeing your thought process and life, this is allowing others to be in charge.

We are told to bring Down - cast Down imaginations and every high thing that exalts itself against the knowledge of GOD, BRINGING EVERY Thought into captivity to the obedience of Christ. Let us once again become a FOCUSED PEOPLE. A people that is.,single-minded in thought and intent. Let us once again have our thinking process renewed. Let us have mental discipline and become focused.

It is a scientific fact we only operate somewhere at ten percent or less of our mental faculty. The other ninety percent is not there just to keep our ears apart, but it is there for a purpose. We need to begin to understand why, what for, and tap into it.

This book you are reading will demand concentration. This will be an activity which will cause you to be or become a critical thinker with mental activity which will cause you to ponder, think, meditate, and produce an appropriate action designed to bring the desired result. If you are not in any kind of mental activity now or in the recent past which is both stimulating and challenging, you will have lost your concentration and memory skills, as some of you already have.

Physiologically, if everything is okay, there is no correlation between aging and memory loss of concentration abilities. Far too many people in their forties and fifties state that they are getting old and that is the reason they feel they cannot concentrate, or they are losing their memory skills.

It is a scientific fact that aging does not necessarily mean a memory loss or the loss of concentration skills. The reason they experience a decrease in concentration skills and their ability to think is not as good as it was, is probably because that they do not use their mind in the way they did when they were younger. Because more than not, when a person gets older, many challenge themselves less and less. They do not use their minds but keep themselves involved in MINDLESS ACTIVITIES.

There is even now neurological evidence as to whether a person has been mentally challenging themselves throughout their lifetime. There are what are called DENDRITES in the brain. Dendrites help communicate with brain cells.

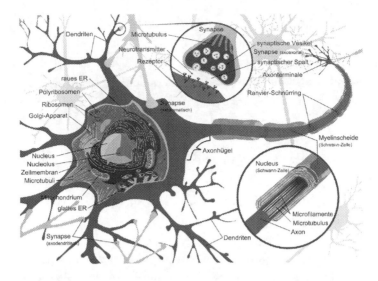

When you do not challenge yourself or use your mind the way you should, these dendrites begin to curl, and the degree of the curl is proportionate to the loss of certain mental abilities.

There is a law of nature, the "USE IT OR LOOSE IT" principle.

Some never use their mind and when autopsy done, they find those peoples brain slick as an onion. When you use your mind, it will be wrinkled and curled. Which do you want?

Our mind is awesome and we humans, or at least most use less than 10% of it.

THIS IS LIFE TO THOSE that WILL CHOOSE TO RECEIVE AND ALLOW THE

PROCESS TO CHANGE THEM. We are on a journey that will lead to an exciting, valuable prize of a life that works on purpose and abundantly with dreams realized. But please, take note. That is not the only prize, but in addition to that prize is the act of learning ...AND LIVING IN THE CREATIVE GOD ZONE abundantly living!

CHAPTER SIX

TRANSFORMANCE BY RENEWING THE MIND

"I beseech you therefore brethren, by the mercies of GOD, that you may present your bodies a living sacrifice, holy, acceptable to GOD which is your reasonable service." (Romans 12:1)

Now, we are talking about physical bodies, But HE goes on to say and which means, hang on, I am not finished. There is more to this that I am sharing. And do not be conformed to this world, but be transformed by the renewing of your mind, that you may prove what is the good and acceptable and perfect will of GOD.

Transformed is a metamorphosis, a change. What do you get transformed by? How do you become transformed? You become transformed by the renewing of your mind, that you may prove what is the good and acceptable and perfect will of GOD.

Most Christians think once you are born again, that is all they needed to do and everything else is automatic. As the youth of today would say, "NOT! ▪

I do not mean to be insulting, but if you were a dork before you were born again, you are just a BORN. AGAIN DORK!! That is all. It changes nothing else. If you want your thinking process changed, to be transformed, to be different, so you can present your body as a living sacrifice, then you will have to do something about the way you think.

There is a Greek word called PSYCHOSOMATIC. Split it in two, you have psycho and soma. Psycho means the mind exerts influence over the soma, the body.

PSYCHOSOMATIC MEAN MIND- INFLUENCE OVER BODY. You will find that psycho, the mind, will try to manifest itself in soma, the body. Long term, the things that you think will manifest in your body, good or bad, positive, or negative.

You can begin to see in our mental process, strongholds are built by CONSTANT REPETITION in the way we think. Take arthritis, for instance. You will find that much of it is caused by rigidity in our thinking. Unbending, unforgiving, uncompromising, but more particular, unforgiving. We are very rigid in our mind, so the body begins to manifest itself in rigidity. Psycho, the mind, will attempt to manifest itself in soma, the body.

That is why it is so important we take charge of our thought process and renew our mind. Begin to focus on good, positive, lovely, joyful, peaceful things. Long term, as we focus on these things, they will begin to manifest in your body and in your life. YOU HAVE THE CHOICE TO CHANGE. Your mind has a tremendous influence over your body. It says, "And do not be conformed to this world-system but be ye transformed." (Romans 12:2A)

Butterflies are beautiful. My son Dean always had the best collection of anyone, of butterflies. He had them all categorized and displayed. But have you ever seen those magnificent butterflies before they go through the crystalline stage, or transformation? They look like ugly, gross little maggots. That is what they look like before they are metamorphosed, or transformed, or changed.

PICTURE EXAMPLE

You too, may be a grub, a maggot, an ugly dog thinking of doom and gloom. And woe is me. But you can have a transformation. You can be metamorphosized. You can become like a beautiful butterfly. I do not mean with fifty face lifts either, like Phyllis Diller.

But rather you can be METAMORPHASIZED BY RENEWING YOUR THOUGHT

PROCESS. When you think health, you manifest health. When you think beauty, you manifest beauty. When think love, you manifest love. When you think about success, you manifest success.

It starts with you making a conscious decision and choice to begin to control your thought process and to renew it daily, so that it can change you. Whatever you sow, that is what you will reap.

Remember the use it or lose it principle? You use it or lose it, for there is nothing going to replenish if you do not use it. That is the scriptural LAW of GOD, the CREATOR. USE it OR LOSE it. Whatever you want, sow it and you will reap it.

The *word renew, the renewing of our mind, means to restore*, make something as it was in the original condition. The original condition of the way we thought it was as Adam thought way back at the creation of mankind, which was before the fall of human race in his original state or relationship between him and his CREATOR.

Now man, unless he is born again, has a fallen nature which is in direct opposition to GOD'S nature. But when one becomes born again and becomes a new creation, he is restored back to the original relationship between him and his GOD/CREATOR through the finished work of JESUS HRIST, the Son of GOD.

JESUS TOOK THE HAND OF FALLEN MAN AND TOOK THE HAND OF GOD AND BROUGHT RECONCILIATION.

Now, we are partakers once again of HIS Divine Nature. And it is so important that we renew our minds, that we learn to do things with our minds.

In the beginning, Adam was a genius. We need to learn how to use our restored and renewed mind. We must learn how to take control over our minds, take control over our thought process.

Daily, we are being bombarded and programmed with negative inputs. If you allow your mind to think and focus on these things, they will manifest in your life. But, if you will choose to do what GOD'S WORD says, GOD'S WORD tells us what to think on.

"Finally, brethren, whatever things are true, noble, just, pure, lovely, of excellent report, if there is any virtue, anything praiseworthy, meditate. Think on these things." (Philippians 4:8-9)

Think on these things. Think means to form in one's mind. Hold in one's mind. Reflect, focus, concentrate. Reflect on these things. Bounce them around continually in your mind. Form them. Focus on them, and psycho, the mind will manifest over soma, the body.

When You become focused on whatsoever is true, honest, just, pure, good report, virtue, praise, peace, joy and positive, these things will develop in your life.

HE just told us in Corinthians that we could bring every thought under HIS captivity. That does not mean you are not to continue to live in the world, quit your job, and move to a monastery somewhere. But HE is saying that you can start to have CONTROL and INFLUENCE over your mind, your thought process. Please note, your standard of thought process should never be what you think, or I think, or anyone else thinks.

It must be what GOD thinks.

I shared a moment ago about thought patterns spiraling down from A to B, the gutter, and How dangerous that is. When that occurs, you are at the point where the enemy is firing at your rapid thinking. Now, as a born-again believer, at that point, it is NOT your responsibility to decide if it is a negative thought pattern, because just that alone can be overwhelming.

It is the PARACLETE, THE HELPER, HOLY Spirit, the one who has been sent, drawn alongside you to lead, guide and direct. It is the HOLY Spirit's responsibility to tell you that it is a negative thought. And when you get that quickening in your spirit, then there is a response you need to make and THAT IS, STOP IT!

You say, "How do you stop thinking about something?" For example, a religious person may say, "I just began to pray in tongues." Well, that is great, but while your mouth is moving, your brain is somewhere else. The enemy is still trying to get into you through your thought pattern. Did you know I can quote Scripture and my mind goes somewhere else? That is double-minded.

Many people in church raise their hands in praise of GOD and are meanwhile thinking about lunch. The reason for this is that GOD the CREATOR has designed and equipped us with a great organ, THE MIND, with which we can do several things at once. But, when the enemy is throwing you thoughts, what you must do is first, stop it.

For example, birds may fly over your head and you cannot stop that, but you can stop them from building a nest there. You have to stop the thoughts. You have the responsibility to replace what the enemy is putting in your mind with something else. AND THAT SOMETHING ELSE SHOULD BE THE WORD OF GOD. Philippians says think on good, just noble thoughts and positive things.

Every time JESUS was tempted, HE said, "It is written ▪

NOW, let me help you. I am not talking about just quoting Scripture, because there are times you are thinking so fast that the last thing you could remember would be a Scriptural reference, anyway. But if you will get THE CONCEPT, then you have got it won.

Remember the concept!

Corporations or businesses will use GODLY concepts. Guess what? They still work. They do not quote the Scriptures for those concepts, but they grasp a hold of the concept.

The definition of concept is an abstract notion, mental impression, a thing conceived, idea, or mental picture.

Some people have problems with self-esteem. They do not feel worthy with nothing worthwhile to say. Even when they get an inspirational thought, the enemy would make it so they never used it. He would say, "IF you do that, people will look at you like you are stupid, so keep your mouth shut." They may go from feeling okay that day to feeling stupid, and they cannot make anything work after that point.

If you can grasp a hold of the things I am sharing, get the concept, and say, 'Wait a minute! Stop when those thought patterns come, (and they will come to all of us), even if you cannot remember the verbatim WORD OF GOD which says, "I have the mind of Christ." Then you can say what GOD thinks and what I think. That may be as close as you get. Point to your head and say, "I have a sound mind. It is okay and solid up there." That is a close version of, "GOD did not give me a spirit to fear, but of power and love and of a sound mind." (1 Timothy 1:7)

It will surprise you because of the concept involved. It will work every time. Then, as you become a little more versed in GOD'S WORD and more sophisticated, it will be easier for you to quote Scripture. Then when the enemy tells you-you are ugly, you can say, "No, I was created in the image of GOD and HIS beauty rests upon me."

You must choose to switch lanes. REPLACE BAD THOUGHTS WITH GOOD THOUGHT. Repent of your old thinking, have a metanoia, a change. Be converted to GOD'S WAY. HIS way is life to all those that find it. Be transformed by renewing your mind. You are the one who must think about something else. You cannot just think about nothing. That is impossible.

I have observed many motivators in our lives, but I have found two greatest, FEAR and FAITH. Both are forces of the spirit. Both are produced in the spirit. IT will depend totally on you of what you allow to be planted in your life.

If you choose to just listen to junk all the time and never do anything about motivating and changing the way you think, just MINDLESS LIVING and mindless activity, then it will never change your life.

NEVER.

Have you ever heard the terminology in computer language, garbage in, garbage out? Garbage in, garbage out. You must build yourself up. Motivate yourself to change. Renew your mind daily and be transformed or changed. Renew your thought process. This is a disciplined lifestyle.

I, myself, can go a few days without renewing my mind and I can see my motivational drive go way down. It is similar to an energy level being drained off your physical body.

The reason many Christians are not motivated is that they put absolutely no time into themselves or their walk with GOD. THEY ARE Lazy. If it does not happen to them automatically, they will put no effort into achieving it. GOD does not bless lazy people. HE does not bless lazy Christians.

NOW, let us not get off the issue we are discussing in this book. I am not talking about losing your salvation. But I am talking about losing your life now. You cannot have a life worth living, or abundantly if you keep your thought process undisciplined, letting it be fed mental poison daily, just running rampant and being influenced by whatever comes down the pike.

THE FORCE OF FEAR IS DESTRUCTIVE AND DEADLY. FEAR IS FOCUSING ON THE WRONG THING. You get into the negative awhile and you will shut DOWN ALL OF YOUR BODY'S HORMONE SYSTEM. YOU SHUT DOWN YOUR OWN IMMUNE SYSTEM. And this is when different sickness, many health issues and problems find an opening into your life. I genuinely believe this.

Now, every one of us has micros. Everyone has germs. Scientists are struggling with the idea why some people are susceptible, and others are not. I believe all you must do is get into fear for a while and you have opened the door, given an entrance to bacteria.

I believe the force of fear is the difference between the ones more susceptible from the ones not. Most diseases are not even caused by bacteria, such as heart attacks, cancer, arthritis, asthma... Most of these diseases are not caused by germs, but by long term wrong patterns of thinking.

Disease is an interesting word. Break it in two and you have *dis-ease*, or lack of peace. "GOD does not give us a spirit of fear, but of power and love and of sound mind." (2 Timothy 1:7)

The FORCE OF FEAR will take your peace. It will cause *DIS-EASE*. It will make you powerless and take your mind and thought process. Fear is deadly. Psycho, the mind, begins to influence itself over soma, the body. Long-term hatred, anger, bitterness. Will begin to break down your body and suppress the body and destroy you.

Fear is destructive. Fear will suppress the anti-bodies in your body. Fear will suppress your hormone system. Fear will kill you. Fear will immobilize you. There are three hundred and sixty-five Scriptures in the WORD OF GOD speaking against fear. Fear is the most destructive force on this planet. Fear will destroy your faith. You cannot have faith and fear. They are opposing forces.

"Fear not," we are instructed over and over throughout the Bible. Fear not. Do not fear. Be anxious for nothing. Do not worry. "Therefore, I say to you, do not worry about your life." (Matthew 6:25A)

Worry comes from the Greek word MERMNAC, which comes from Merizo, meaning to divide into parts.

The word suggests a distraction, a preoccupation with things that cause anxiety, stress, nervousness and pressure.

ALLOWING WORD THOUGHT PATTERNS TO DIVIDE YOU. We are told not to do that. Do not allow it! But rather, we are instructed to think on whatsoever things are lovely, just, and pure. To rejoice. have joy, peace, and love. We are to think on the positive.

"GOD did not give us a spirit of fear, but of power, love and a sound mind." (II Timothy 1:7))

We have been given a sound mind, which comes from the Greek word SOPHRONIMOS, which is a combination of SOS, safe and PHREN the mind. Hence, safe thinking. Safe thinking which denotes righteous judgment, disciplined thought patterns and the ability to understand and make a right decision, which includes qualities of self- control and self-discipline.

You are to choose what you focus on and think on. You must decide to renew your thought process daily to the WORD OF GOD. 'We must think on whatever things are true, noble and honest." (Philippians 4:8) Honest things are free from error. They are truthful.

Did you know your emotions lie to you? Your emotions are fickle and do not line up with honesty. And we are instructed to think of true, noble, honest things. We are not to live by our emotions or feelings, but the WORD OF GOD. Think on those things.

Look at this that will make the point clearer:

My younger daughter, Tina, is in aviation in the US Navy air. They trained traffic control and her to use instruments. When airline pilots are trained, the very first thing they tell them is "You fly by the instruments, not your emotions or feelings." A pilot flying gets into a storm and gets flipped every which way. Now, his emotions tell him he is okay and flying right. At that point he has two choices; *fly by what the instrument panel says* or go with his emotions. If he goes with his emotions, he is dead.

Emotions will tell you one thing when it is another. Isn't that true? Instructors for pilots hammer it into them. "You fly by the instruments, fly by the instruments!" You fly by your emotions and you are dead. That is why they call it pilot error, because sometimes pilots go by their emotions and their emotions lie to them. We are to live by GOD'S WORD and faith in it and not by what we feel. Our feelings or emotions will lie to us.

In a man's eyes, he is always right, but it brings death. We are not to follow our feelings. But what does GOD'S WORD say? Our mind has outstanding power. Our mind can cure effectively or can kill. You are being programmed daily. Most are being programmed in the negative.

Some of us have been damaged in our thought process more than others. But the Bible clearly teaches that we need to unlearn SOME of that negative garbage and pull down some of those strongholds. Renew ·our minds to what GOD'S positive, good WORD says.

The Bible says to the weak to say, "I am strong." We are to think on the positive, the good. What you think is what will manifest (Psychosomatic).

The Bible says that by HIS stripes we are healed. But the world tells us we are sick and getting sicker. That is why most people, including Christians, are sick. They believe what they watch on television and hear through the media. Such negative advertisement is programming you to get sick.

'When you get a headache, reach for (NAME OF BRAND), or "Fifty percent of you watching this will develop cancer." They constantly put it out there. You will begin to believe it.

Breast cancer, skin cancer, prostate cancer, lung cancer... You say they are just warning you. Maybe they are. But you can become "INSIDIOUSLY PROGRAMMED." You start to think and expect it. The Bible says we need to be transformed or changed by the renewing of our minds." Blessed is the man who walks not in the counsel of the ungodly, nor stands in the path of sinners, nor sits in the seat of the scornful." (Psalm 1:1)

Blessed means happy, successful, prosperous. Do you want to be blessed? HE says we are not to walk in the counsel of the ungodly psychiatrist if we want to be blessed. The choice is mine to go or-not to go and if I choose to go; HE says l will not be blessed.

"But HIS delight is in the law of the LORD, and he meditates day and night." (Psalm 1:2)

The word delight is a remarkably interesting word. It has an intensity to it. When we think of the word delight, we think of watercolor ponies and circuses, or Mary Poppins. But rather DELIGHT HAS AN INTENSITY OF EMOTION!!

The word law could better be translated the WORD of GOD, because they only had a few books back then. We are to meditate on the WORD OF GOD. Do not be afraid of the word meditation. GOD wants you to know' meditation was in HIS WORD a lot longer than when all the weirdos picked it up and perverted it with eastern religion, new age, or weird science.

The Scripture connotation of meditation is to take the WORD OF GOD, revolve it over, reflect it over and over in your mind. Concentrate, focus, say it first thing in the morning and the last at night. By doing that you are beginning to bring thoughts captive. That is what your mind will focus on. Focus on the WORD OF GOD. Allow peace that passes all understanding that comes from GOD through HIS WORD into your mind and manifest in your life.

DO NOT FOCUS OR THINK ON YOUR PROBLEMS. Meditate. Or for a better word, self-talk. Every one of us communicates with each other with few words. But with ourselves, many words. Right now, you are communicating with yourself. I like this information, or I do not. I will do it, or I won't. I receive it or I do not. I am hungry. I am cold....

Now, what the challenge is, is to bring that self-talk in line with the WORD OF GOD. It must be renewed. So instead of our self-talk demoting us, putting us down, or discouraging us, by having it renewed it will begin to lift us up, to motivate us. The Bible says, your mind, your self-talk can be brought under subjection unto the WORD OF GOD. And when you start to do that, this will apply.

"He shall be like a tree planted by the rivers of water that brings forth its fruit in its season, whose leaf also shall not wither, and whatever he does shall prosper." (Psalm 1:3)

Whatsoever you do in business, marriage, investments, ministry, health, school, relationships, etc. If you can attain the goal to bring your self-talk under the WORD OF GOD, then and only then the blessings will flow. This is the truth. We must choose to think positive, good thoughts, thoughts that line up with the WORD OF GOO. THINK WHAT GOD THINKS. Renew our minds daily.

Remember the example of the test on concentration and how the stimulus of our society has insidiously removed our ability to concentrate and focus. For as we head further into the decade of 2021, you will see this type of bombardment on your mind greatly increase. The only way we will be able to stand this is to renew our minds. Renew your thought process daily to the WORD OF GOD.

The common weakness I find today is *the IDLE MIND*, a disconnected mind, a mind not occupied, running disconnected so that the power is not used. IDLE. Your mind is powerful when it is connected and focused. And if you do not take control of your mind, someone or something will·. We must decide to live lie on purpose. We must decide to discipline our lives, to take control of our thoughts. Beginning today, right where you are, you choose.

Karl Marx is a man who started Communism. I dislike what he stood for, but he said something that I do like. He said, *"You listen to something I said once, and you may pick up an odd point. You listen to me five to ten times and you may remember a few points. You listen to me fifty times and you are mine forever. Forever."* This man knew what he was talking about.

HOW much more comes with the WORD OF GOD. Faith or change comes by hearing and hearing by the WORD OF GOD. Delight in, begin to want the WORD OF GOD with an intensity and be transformed or changed by the renewing of your mind and thought process to the WORD OF GOD.

Cast down imaginations and every chief thing that exalts itself against the knowledge of GOD. Bring every thought and emotion into captivity to the obedience of Christ. Take control of your thoughts and renew the mind to the WORD OF GOD. For we do not walk in the flesh, by our senses or emotions, but according to the WORD OF GOD.

Course of Action

Read this chapter until you understand it.

Take/write notes in the margin areas. This will increase your retention rate by seven times.

If you want seven times seven longer retention rate, take the minor points, meditate them day and night over and over until they are internalized.

Research shows everything you are reading right now, that twenty. Five percent will be gone within twenty, Four hours. Within two days, sixty percent will be gone, and by the end of a week, ninety percent will be gone. So, you choose to take the appropriate action based on the WORD OF GOD and see the results that follow.

Remember, if you think you are broken, you are. If you dare not, you do not. If you want to win, but you think you cannot, it is almost a cinch you won't. If you think you will lose, you have lost. For in the world, we find success begins with a fellow's will.

It is all in the state of mind. If you think your outclassed, you are. You have got to think high to rise. You have got to be sure of yourself before you can ever win a prize. Life's battles do not always go to the swiftest or the strongest man. But eventually, the man who wins is the man who thinks he can.

"As a man thinketh in his heart, so is he." (Proverbs 23:7)

ENTER THE CREATIVE GOD ZONE

CHAPTER SEVEN

FIRST THINGS FIRST

JESUS answered him. The first of all commandments is: *"Hear O' Israel, the LORD our GOD, the LORD is one. And you shall love the LORD your GOD with all your heart, with all your soul, and with all your mind."* (Mark 12:29-30)

This is the first commandment. We are to love the LORD with our being; SPIRIT, BODY, SOUL, and all of our mind. And included in that word mind; is DIANOIA, imagination, the eyes of the spirit realm. We must renew our minds daily to the WORD OF GOD, for it is only the WORD OF GOD that will differentiate the word of your SOUL, YOUR Spirit, THE ENEMY, AND THE VOICE OF THE HOLY Spirit.

Just the WORD OF GOD will build us up to a place where we can tune our ears and hear what the Holy Spirit is saying. JESUS said, "My sheep will know my voice and another they will not follow." But it takes practice and discipline to allow the WORD OF GOD first place in your life. YOU CHOOSE!

"The WORD OF GOD is powerful, quick, and sharper than any two-edged sword piercing even to the dividing asunder of soul and spirit and of joints and marrow, and is a discerner of thought and intents of the heart." (Hebrew 4:12)

The word OF GOD is powerful. We must all come to the point where we can say. "I thank GOD through JESUS CHRIST our LORD! So then,

WITH THE MIND, I serve the law of God, but with the flesh, the law of sin." (Romans 7:25)

Where do you think, in your brain or mind? There are sixty trillion cells in my body, one hundred billion in my brain alone. I choose to access the WORD OF GOD to permeate every cell in my brain. I want to renew my mind to the WORD OF GOD because I know it will change me when I do. I will enter the CREATIVE ZONE of God.

I will tell you flat out that you are responsible for the decisions you make. You are the sum total of the decision you have already made. You must decide today to begin this journey of learning with an open mind and a willingness to follow the instruction. You must understand where the heart is that you give to JESUS to be your LORD. You must realize you are responsible for the decisions you make. I want you to know where your heart is that you give to GOD. The place where your heart is that is the CREATIVE ZONE, the area, the issues, or force of life flow, or better understood, the results of your life!

Early in the book of Genesis, when Satan came to Eve to deceive her, the Bible says, "The serpent was more cunning than any other beast of the field." (Genesis 3:1) He said to Eve, "Has GOD indeed said you shall not eat of every tree of the garden?" Satan came to her mind, to reason and to influence her imagination. He beguiled her, seduced.

He knew exactly what to say. He was basically telling her, "God does not mean what HE says." And that is the same strategy he uses on men and women today in decades of the the2020s. THE definition OF THE HEART IN YOUR CHEST IS THAT it IS THE ORGAN THAT RECYCLES AND PUMPS BLOOD THROUGHOUT THE BODY AND THROUGHOUT THE VEINS, ONE TIME EVERY MINUTE.

THAT IS Responsibility OF HEART, TO RECYCLE YOUR BLOOD on time, AS it WAS DESIGNED BY GOD, THE CREATOR.

But is that the heart we give to GOD and make a confession in JESUS CHRIST? NO! It is not!

I will tell you where it is. JESUS' number one warning for the very last days, "Do not be deceived."

And I have found a great deception in the world and have been taught and passed down through religious seminars and the secular world for centuries. That deceptive teaching is where the heart is, we give to GOD.

Please understand that the battles of life are primarily fought and won or lost in mind. That is where Satan always comes to the mind. Not your feet, elbow, or teeth, but your mind. THE MIND IS POWERFUL. We, humans, are a three-part being.

We are SPIRIT. We have a SOUL and live in a BODY.

The soul comprises MIND, WILL, EMOTION, AND INTELLECT, and IMAGINATION.

The Scriptures tell us we must love the LORD GOD with all our soul and mind (imagination). You must renew your mind daily to the WORD OF GOD. Then and only then can you be transformed or changed.

You say, "It sounds like you are teaching mind over matter."

Well, look at it this way. I (you) have the mind of CHRIST over any matter the devil brings up; therefore, it does not matter.

We were created to win at life. Please quit hiding your head in the sand when it comes to the subject of the mind. By doing that, we have allowed everyone and everything to take over the mind, from Scientology, Christian science, moral clarification, humanism... I could go on and on.

Christians, mostly, have been passive in the mind's area. We have just folded our hands, blindfolded our eyes, and we have lost. We are losing significantly. But not anymore! The subject of the mind is being taken back for the Kingdom of our God and of HIS CHRIST.

The WORD OF GOD says be changed, transformed by renewing your mind to the WORD OF GOD. We have been so bombarded with wrong teaching, and as a whole, we have accepted it to be the truth. As we go into the CREATIVE ZONE, you must let go of all your past teaching and be ready to be retaught after the fact. WE WILL UNLEARN MUCH AND RELEARN MORE. (Not all past education was wrong, so you hang onto that and add this to your foundation of faith.)

Too much false teaching causes incorrect responses, and therefore, terrible results.

Beginning with Aristotle, the Greek Philosopher who teamed up with Plato in Macedonia, Greece, three hundred and fifty years before Christ, Aristotle credited in his philosophy the heart of the chest as sensing and thinking. And he credited the brain as the cooling of the blood. The only problem he had it reversed!

And "shifty Satan" has used that from the beginning of man's time to deceive the world, to destroy the message of truth, to negate the instructions or the how we connect with GOD. And we, by and large, have become a disconnected people with no power. The entire world needs to read this book and hear the message of the ages penned on these papers.

You must learn how the Kingdom of God operates. You must LEARN HOW TO CONNECT TO GOD THE CREATOR, how to enter the CREATIVE ZONE, and make life work.

Do you, my dear reader, know where the heart of the mind is? See, no one can argue with the fact the heart organ in the chest recycles and pumps the blood.

You will find in the Scriptures the word heart is mentioned eight hundred and thirty-one times. Today, in the decade of the 2020s, if you are going to survive, you are going to have to have more than sensationalism, emotionalism, or inspiration. Those are all good and needed, BUT YOU NEED INFORMATION. Because what you do not know in the Kingdom of God will hurt you. "Wisdom and knowledge will be the stability of your times and the strength of salvation." (Isaiah 33:SA) "Always learning and never able to come to the knowledge of the truth." (II Timothy 3:7)

And that word knowledge of GOD comes from a Greek word, *EPIGNOSIS*.

Epignosis means we have never come to the full discernment of the truth of who we are in our relationship with God, the Almighty. "Now the Spirit (Holy Spirit) expressly says that in later times _some will depart from the faith, giving heed to deceiving spirits and doctrines of demons." (I Timothy 4:1) You will hear many voices on the earth, and many voices will cause confusion.

The Bible says GOD is not the author of confusion, but rather HE gives you power, love, and a sound mind. But you will be the one who chooses to have your mind renewed to the truth of the WORD OF GOD.

Quit listening to everything that comes your way. Learn how to discern truth from deception. "Solid food belongs to those who are full age. That is those who, because of use, have their senses developed to discern both good and evil." (Hebrews 5:14)

In other words, you better grow up and quit acting like a baby. You better become mature (not in years) and be in full knowledge and skillful, knowing right from wrong, truth from deception.

It says YOU. Exercise your senses so that you can discern good from evil. Some people I know must believe everybody and everything they hear. They are so confused about life, unfocused, disconnected, and wonder why nothing ever works in their life. What needs to happen is, you better get your mind in correlation, and get your mind in line with GOD'S mind, or else Satan, the father of all lies, the master deceiver, is going to come and the things you used to think were wrong and you will gradually be led to think, "Oh, that is not so bad." You may not take part in those Things, but you will be so compromised that you allow for those things. You will have no spiritual discernment to know right and wrong in the world anymore.

The WORD says exercise your senses. The Greek meaning for your senses is that organ that is used for perception, the mind. "I thank GOD through JESUS CHRIST, our Lord! So then with the mind, I myself serve the law of GOD, but with the flesh, the law of sin. (Romans 7:25) "Your word I have hidden in my heart that I might not sin against you." (Psalm 119:11)

Now, understand what HE is telling us. Remember, HE is not talking about your heart, the blood pump that recycles your blood. HE says, "I have hidden in my heart."

The word heart comes from Hebrew word, *LEBLEBAB,* which means my will and my intellect. (That is in your soul realm and part of your mind.)

That is where I have hidden it, that I may not sin against GOD. What makes us human-beings think that the WORD OF GOD is so abstract, and we hide it down somewhere in our blood-pump area.

What most know and call their heart. But yet the battle is always in your mind. That is where it starts and really ends. So, when attacks come to our mind, we do not know the word of truth to combat the attack, because to us, it is so abstract, and we hide it down in our chest cavity somewhere and we do not know where it is... Cannot find it with a FBI search warrant and hound dog.

For example, it is the same as knowing how much money you have in the bank or knowing the name of each child you have. Come on and see what I am sharing. You are to hide the WORD OF GOD in your heart, which is your will and intellect, a specific place. Where do you think? Your brain' mind? There are sixty trillion cells in my body, one hundred billion in my brain alone. And I want every one of those cells to have a scripture in it. I want to hide the WORD OF GOD there. I want to renew my mind to the WORD OF GOD and when I do, I shall be transformed or changed. "Therefore, we do not lose heart, even though our outward man is perishing, and the inward man is being renewed day by day." (II Corinthians 4:16)

When you can get the WORD OF GOD truly hidden in your heart (mind, will, emotion, intellect), then when the enemy comes against you, no matter what form he takes and tells you that you are a loser, ugly, fat, no good, never will make it, this is it, or that you will never recognize your dream and he makes you feel really bad about yourself, if you know the word, if you have it hidden in your heart, you will look at that negative adversary attacking you and say, "Oh no, I have the mind of a twenty-year-old person. I just do not have the body, but I am changing. I am a winner. I am what I am because I serve the Great, I AM, (GOD). So, get out of my face."

"For as he thinks in his heart, so is he." (Proverbs 23:7) Where do you think? MIND/BRAIN? That if you confess with your mouth, the Lord JESUS and believe in your heart that GOD has raised HIM from the dead, you will be saved. For with the heart one believes unto righteousness, and with the mouth confession is made unto salvation. (Romans 10:9- 10) Where do you believe?

It SAYS THE HEART, AND IS TRANSLATED MIND/BRAIN; WILL INTELLECT, AND EMOTION. You think there, in your heart; mind, will, emotion. You believe there in your heart; mind, will, emotion. Don't you think it is time you quit letting the enemy, Satan, make an oaf out of you? I am not being disrespectful.

Paul says, "Brethren, I would not have you ignorant." I say, "Thank you, Paul. I don't want to be ignorant." See, there is a big difference between ignorance and stupidity. Ignorance is, you just did not know the information that you needed. But once you learned it, you weren't ignorant in that area anymore. Stupid means either you cannot or will not learn.

So, you need to quit being ignorant. You need to quit letting the devil make an oaf out of you. Do you know what an oaf is? It is a dumb, ignorant person and a jerk. The devil has made jerks out of us because he thinks we are dumb. Did you know the Bible says, "My people are destroyed for lack of knowledge, because you have rejected knowledge." (Hosea 4:6)

Are you ready for a change? Are you ready to see the way life should be? Because what you see is what you will get, (WYSISYG Principle). So, we must change what you think on, focus on and enter the CREATIVE ZONE. "For to be carnally minded is death, but to be spiritually minded is life and peace." (Romans 8:6) So what are you thinking about? Are you carnally minded or are you spiritually minded, which is life and peace? You have the choice of what you habitually think on. No, you CANNOT CONTROL YOUR THOUGHTS. For example, you cannot stop a bird from flying over your head, but you can stop him from building a nest there. It is your choice. The way the anti-christ is loose in our world, seducing spirits are let loose to wear down the saints of the most high GOD.

just as the Book of Revelation and the Book of Daniel speak of seducing spirits, are coming to the minds of people and wearing them down, wearing them out! I have never known a day when people are just flat worn out. Such hopelessness, no fight left, no dreams or vision, no creativeness.

Doctors' offices are filled with tired people. They are worn out, filled with fear, great fears of all kinds. You see, a man or woman who starts out with a right attitude in their ministry or whatever and ends up fallen or shipwrecked. Why? Seducing spirits lured them into wrong things, filling their minds with wrong pictures, videos, thoughts, causing them to become unfocused and disconnected.

Some of the greatest roads of the seducing spirits work through movies, videos, pornography books. You, my dear friend, will have to choose what you look at. King David in the Old Testament said, "I will set no evil before my eyes." He knew the principle of what you see is what you get. He Knows that what you feed your mind continually you will end up with.

You are going to have to choose what you are going to do when seducing spirits come against you. For they will come with insidious thoughts. And you will have what you will end up with. And you will have to decide with the heart of your mind; your will and intellect and what comes into your thought process, what you give access to.

Nobody becomes a loser overnight. So, in essence, you must quit letting Satan and his attacks harass your mind. YOU HAVE TO UNDERSTAND WHERE YOUR HEART IS. Do you know where your heart is? See, the human body has sixty trillion cells in it and one hundred billion in the brain.

"My son, given attention to my words, incline your ears to my sayings." (Proverbs 4:20) Let me ask, where do you attend to HIS WORDS? Point to your mind. Right there. What are you to incline? Your ears. Incline your ears to what I am saying. But here is where most people go wrong. Do NOT let him depart from your eyes. Keep them in the midst of your heart. When you say, keep them in the midst of your heart, most people are talking about the place of their bodies called the viscera section, which is the place that houses the lungs and heart in the chest.

In other words, your guts. Let me tell this story. There was a little girl in Sunday school, and they had been teaching about asking JESUS to come and live in your heart. So, one day at the dinner table this little child asked her mom, "Mom, does JESUS live in our heart?" Her mom answered very cautiously as she really did not know what her five-year-old was getting at. "Yes, JESUS lives in our heart." The little girl pointed to the center of her chest area and stomach and said, "Does JESUS live way down here?" Her mom said, "Yes." The little girl answered, "Here with all the spaghetti and ice cream?" See, it is obvious in our understanding the relating to it, there is a problem, because there is no little man living down there. (Point to your viscera section.)

Please, understand this chapter of this book. Keep your heart. Keep your will. YOU MUST SERVE GOD BY CHOICE, not to please anyone else, but you choose. And when you serve him by choice, your will is involved. "Do not let them depart from your eyes. Keep them in the midst of your heart.

For they are life to those who find them and health to all their flesh. Keep your heart with diligence for out of it springs the issues of life." (Proverbs 4:21-23) You must, above all, keep your heart, your will and your intellect. Keep your heart. Guard it, because out of it will flow the issue of life, or more aptly, the results. There is no body whoever committed murder, adultery, or anything without it first being in the mind. With THE HEART OF THE MIND, the will, the intellect.

The heart means the core, the middle, the essence. So where do you make the decisions? That is the place. The Bible says guard that place! Because out of it, out of the heart flows the issues, the decisions that bring results in your life. The Hebrew word for issues is TOTSAAH, which means results. Please, hear and understand out of the heart flow results of what you do. If this generation does not learn where the heart is that they give GOD, they are doomed.

Serving GOD is not some kind of abstract life, but in reality, a relationship. If you can get someone to give their will to GOD, then you will have the rest of them. GOD has left us free will moral agents in the sense that we have full use of our will power and choice. GOD wants you to freely serve HIM. Line your will up with HIS will. That power is in your hand to choose. And then when you choose to serve HIM, you will do right, you will talk right, and you will to be right. Then there is a supernatural power that I cannot explain. That comes AFTER you choose. GOD has always used this law of reciprocity in the Bible. GOD says, "You draw nigh to me and I draw nigh to you." Now, I can't explain this. No one can. But it is true, none the less. When you look up with the heart of the mind and say, "GOD, I need you, "then there is an electrifying supernatural Power that comes from Heaven to help you accomplish what you have set out to do. THAT IS GRACE! Grace: The power and ability to accomplish what GOD tells you.

This is truth. Please, grasp it. Understand it and it shall make you free.

Aren't you tired of being undecided? I was. That is why I searched and found the truth. I wanted life to work, and it does work. "But I fear, lest somehow, as the serpent deceived EVE by his craftiness. So, your minds may be corrupted from the simplicity that is CHRIST." (II Corinthians 11:3)

The Greek word for corrupted comes from PHTHEIRO, which means to waste away, to be ruined by moral influences. Our society is full of the product of wrong thinking. Child molestation influences, aids, adultery, murder, abortion, stealing, immorality of all kinds. These are all end results to wrong thinking! "For GOD did not send HIS son into the world to condemn the world, but that the world through HIM might be saved." (John 3:17)

The reason it says, "might be saved" is because your will and choice is involved to believe and accept what JESUS CHRIST was sent to do, did and finished, and now sits at the FATHER'S right hand of power and authority. "For GOD so loved the world that HE gave HIS only begotten son, so that whoever believes in HIM (something you choose to do) should not perish but have everlasting life." (John 3:16)J

The world in Greek is KOSMOS. Kosmos means this earth, solar system, and all that is in it - mankind, which is the adornment and its social structure. That is what GOD loved so much, was the kosmos, the whole thing.

And HE says HE did not send HIS son into the kosmos (the whole thing) to condemn the world. The Greek word for condemn is KRINO. Krino means to mentally or judicially damn you.

GOD ALMIGHTY sent HIS son, JESUS down. (He descended before he could ascend.) "Then the multitudes who went before and those who needed a Savior, cried out saying, 'Hosanna be to the son of David! Blessed he who comes in the name of the Lord! Hosanna is the highest!'" (Matthew 21:9) They cried, "Hosanna, Hosanna, Hosanna!" Do you know what Hosanna means in Greek? Hosanna. (Just kidding.)

Hosanna means a declaration, AN Exclamation THAT SOMEONE VERY SPECIAL IS COMING BY. And if you trace this word back, you will find that the word Hosanna goes back to the original in the Old Testament, which is YASHEUA. Yasheua means here comes GOD'S love in action to redeem me back both mentally and spiritually to GOD ALMIGHTY.

It was Satan that came to Eve in the garden and broke her will down. And when he broke her will down, she gave in and listened to what Satan said. Satan basically said, 'You do not have to believe GOD." Satan came to her MIND, seduced her, broke her will down and she gave in. He came through her imagination, her creative side and said, and she believed a lie.

And that is basically why the world is a mess now. One thing you need to get settled in your mind and get settled right now, you must have faith in GOD. That faith is incubated - housed in your MIND. Without faith, it is impossible to please GOD. And faith will come by hearing and hearing, by the WORD OF GOD. And you shall be transformed. That transformation comes by the RENEWING OF YOUR MIND to the WORD OF GOD. You have to determine in your mind. You have to purpose in the heart of your mind. You, not anyone else, but you. You must make the choice. Folks, if you have been having it bad and it looks like it is going to get worse, it probably will. Your faith will be tested to the max. The world is in a perilous state. It is as if Satan is working overtime from your destruction and demise, and he is. But just as they said when they saw JESUS coming, "Here comes GOD'S love in action." JESUS is the ALPHA AND OMEGA, A to Z. All hope is in Him and His Word.

And JESUS has come to restore all that will allow Him access, to restore them, to restore your sanity, to restore you back to the CREATIVE ZONE of life. That is what Satan broke down in the garden, to keep MANKIND POWERLESS.

And Apostle Paul understood that and said, "I fear, as Satan hath beguiled Eve, he will corrupt your mind with simplicity." All you have to do is listen to what the humanists say, what the Satanist say. Listen to moral clarification that is in our school system that says, to make up your own rules. That means no rules to go by. Is that a bunch of crock or what?

Honey, one thing you had better learn and know and understand, GOD ALMIGHTY has got some rules and laws in HIS book. And it does not matter what echelon of life you come from. IF YOU DISOBEY THE LAW YOU WILL PAY FOR IT. When you open your mind up to Satan, he will drive you, drive you wild, take your sanity. And he is not respecter of persons. He does not care whether you are rich or poor, black, or white, bonded or free, Greek or Jew, male or female. To him, it does not matter. It does not matter what echelon of life you come from. If you do not learn where your heart is, and you do not learn self-control. If you do not learn to make the right decisions, you are opening yourself for Satan to come into your .mind and send you to mental institutions and psychiatric wards.

You will have more problems than you know what to do with. If you will, listen to what I am sharing and make the right choice. And you choose to cover your life with the blood of JESUS every day. You must apply the blood to your MIND and to your choices. And GOD will keep you in a sane mind the rest of your life. ISN'T THAT GOOD NEWS!! Good news, that is the best news.

GOD loves you. You are incredibly special. But you must have WISDOM and KNOWLEDGE. There are many men and women that were special. They have fallen like arrows shot in the wind and hit the ground and missed the mark terribly.

These were young people that got out into the world and their peer pressure and influence and seducing spirits took them into things that were immoral, illicit and against GOD'S laws. They were prayed for, loved, and even in some circles, they tried to cast out demons and deliver these folks, but failed to teach truth that make free.

But one very young girl that was diagnosed with aids said before she passed away, in a very weak voice, "IF THEY WOULD HAVE TAUGHT ME WHERE MY HEART WAS, I WOULD NOT HAVE DIED OF AIDS. BUT THE CHURCH I WAS IN, THEY PRAYED FOR ME, CAST THE DEVIL OUT, BUT THEY NEVER TOLD ME I WAS RESPONSIBLE FOR THE DECISIONS I MADE." You may never meet me personally, but I want you to know where your heart is, where your heart is that you give to GOD, where your heart is.

That is the place the issues of life flow from. And anytime you have a battle, it comes to your MIND. Anytime you get depressed, oppressed, the attacks will come right here to your mind. And with the heart of the mind which is located in the cerebrum part of the brain.

GOD made your brain. GOD wants you to use your brain. You were made in HIS image. "For you formed my inward parts, you covered me in my mother's womb. I will praise you for I am fearfully and wonderfully made. Marvelous are your works and that my SOUL knows very well." (Psalm 139:14-14) GOD made you! There are no two of us alike. Each has their own DNA. GOD DID NOT MAKE US LIKE ROBOTS. HE GAVE US A CHOICE. WE HAVE POWEROF CHOICE. GOD put HIS spirit in us. HE created us and breathed into us. He breathed HIS spirit, the life of GOD. HE put that in us. "And the LORD, our GOD formed man of the dust of the ground, and breathed into his nostrils the breath of life, and man became a living being." (Genesis 2:7, 1:26-27) GOD put that breath in us -HIS spirit. THAT SPIRIT ACTIVATED OUR MINDS TO THINK, the very spirit of GOD, the breath, the life of GOD.

GOD gave you that life, but he gave you a choice. You could use your life to bless HIM or damn HIM. I is your choice.

SEE, GENUINE LOVE CANNOT EX1ST UNLESS IT IS FREELY GIVEN. GOD does not demand that you love HIM. You choose to freely give your love. I thank GOO through JESUS CHRIST our LORD! So then, with the MIND, "I myself serve the law of GOD, but with the flesh, the law of sin." (Romans 7:25)

With my mind, I choose to serve the law of GOD. The law simply means the precepts, the commands of GOD. HE says, "Don't lie," then do not lie! HE says "Don' t worry. I am going to take care of you. Don't worry!" Do you really believe HIM, or will most of you reading this book continue to worry? If you choose to continue to worry, you are opening yourself up to all kinds of problems, mentally, physically, and spiritually. If GOD'S WORD says something for your sake, believe it. CHOOSE WITH YOUR MIND TO SERVE THE LAW OF GOD. Why do Christians and the church world as a whole think GOD saved us to be robots and never give credence to our mind after salvation? But there is so much in the Bible about your MIND. Your mind is powerful. GOD wants you to serve HIM with your mind. Line your will up with HIS will. GOD created your mind. GOD loves your mind and GOD wants you to use your mind.

Many reading this book need to repent from their old way of Ilc, old way of living and old way of conversation. You need to respond. Most people think repent means, "I go to an altar someplace and cry and say am sorry for all I have done wrong or have not done." They beat, scream, kick, holler and yell. And they call that repentance. It is like the criminal cries and says he is sorry, but really, he is sorry he got caught.

Repent comes from the Greek word METANOIA, which means to change your mind, to think differently and to reconsider and go another way. It is like a joumey. If you are on a train to a certain destination and you are not getting there, get on another train. Do it differently. Reconsider.

YOU MAKE THE CHOICE. GOD loves you. GOD only has good for you in mind. So please, get that in your mind. GOD loves you! GOD loves you!!!

The decade of the eighties has left us with doctors out our gazoo and psychologists telling us we need our emotions healed. Recommending books about healing of the emotions, seminars, group sessions, to let us look at our emotions. Well, that is all fine and good. But healing our emotions is like bandaging an artery cut. You are trying to treat a symptom and ignoring the cause.

WHAT ARE YOUR EMOTIONS? EMOTIONS ARE FEELINGS. You do not need your feelings healed; you need what caused the feeling healed. Emotions are feelings. Books have bombarded the Christian bookstores and secular bookstores on how to heal your emotions, but if you get your mind healed, your emotions are going to be all right.

Yes! You may quote me! You may give a copy of this book to your therapist. Let us get down to the ROOT CAUSES. For example, it is like the guy down south who would go every Sunday down at the alter and pray for GOD to get the cobwebs out of his mind. He would do that every service. But one Sunday they had an incredibly wise gentleman conduct the service. That old guy came down and began to pray, "Oh GOD, get the cobwebs out of my mind." The wise old preacher went by, laid hands on him, and said, "GOD, kill the spider!" Get the root cause and the cobwebs will disappear. And we are all screaming, "GOD, heal my emotions." In reality your emotions are feeling from what went on up here in your mind.

Let's get to the root causes and our emotions will fall in line. For example, I could talk about fleas and have all of you scratching from head to toe. I could talk about eating a lemon and you would all pucker. I could talk about yawning or yawn in front of you and you would yawn. Those are feelings. We have feelings, but we are not to live by feelings alone. (Feelings are a part of our makeup and feelings are good. But they are fickle, and you cannot live on them.) We need our minds healed. WE NEED TO LEARN TO MAKE RIGHT CHOICES. WE NEED TO MAKE RIGHT DECISIONS.

Satan's plan of attack, his strategy, is to come and weaken and dilute your faith and to make you inoperative, to get you on high center where you cannot go forward or backwards. "Now, faith is the substance of things hoped for, the evidence of things not seen." (Hebrews 11:1) "But without faith it is impossible to please HIM, for he who comes to GOD must believe that HE is and that HE is a rewarder of those who diligently seek

HIM." (Hebrews 11:6) 'Who are kept by the power of GOD through faith for salvation ready to be revealed at the last time." (I Peter 1:5) We are kept by the power of GOD through faith.

Kept is a Greek word PHROUREW, which means a military term picturing a sentry standing guard as protection against the enemy "We are in spiritual combat, but GOD'S power and peace are sentinels. (Philippians 4:7) We are kept by the power of GOD through faith.

Now, where is faith incubated? Your foot, your elbow, your blood pump? No! "That CHRIST may dwell in your hearts through faith; that you are being rooted and grounded in love." (Ephesians 3:17)

That CHRIST may dwell in your heart by faith, your heart, the seat of the real you. 'Who having not seen you love, though now you do not see HIM, yet believing, you rejoice with joy inexpressibly and full of glory." (I Peter 1:8) This says how can you love a GOD whom you have not seen. We have never seen HIM, but we love HIM. We believe HIM.

That is by faith. And faith comes by hearing and hearing the WORD OF GOD. The Bible says, "Confess with your mouth and believe in your heart that HE is the son of the living GOD." By faith, I believe and love somebody I have never see. I do that by faith. FAITH IS A GREEK WORD PISTAS, WHICH MEANS THREE THINGS.

Please always remember this and set it firmly in your mind. Without faith you cannot please GOD. Without faith you will not make it.

FIRST, faith means I believe GOD.

SECOND, faith means I am going to trust HIM.

THIRDLY, faith means fidelity. And fidelity is the opposite of infidelity, which means when times get tough, I am not going to go seek another lover. YOU MUST DECIDE AND SAY I PLEDGE MY FIDELITY TO GOD!

You need to quit letting Satan harass you, saying if you had faith you would be healed. You have got to make your mind up. If I never get healed I pledge my fidelity to GOD, because when I step in glory, I will have a glorified body. The Bible says the only way you can please GOD is by faith. It does not matter where you are, how tough times are, pledge your fidelity to GOD. I have! The GOD we serve is a GOOD GOD and HE wants you renewed for good things to come out of you, learning how HIS kingdom operates, and you are walking in the CREATIVEZONE. "Fight the good fight of faith. Lay hold on eternal life to which you were also called and have confessed the good confession in the presence of many witnesses." (I Timothy 6:12)

You will have to fight a good fight of faith. A good fight is the one you win. I know how hard it is to look up and say, "GOD, I believe you." when you do not see the evidence of anything. You must say, "GOD, I am going to trust you." Believe and confess. EVEN WHEN TIMES GET Tough, DO NOT VOICE OPPOSITION TO GOD. That is one of the worst things you could do. It is so important to choose to watch what you are thinking and what you are saying. What you say and what you think will determine the way you walk and live. It is your choice. You make your own decisions. Numerous times I have had to fight the good fight of faith.

The Greek word for fight is AGONIZOMI, which means to struggle. There are times in your life you will have to struggle. It will not always be easy. You are going to have to fight for your faith. Agonizomi means to contend, which there will be times when you will have to duel, argue, quarrel. It also means you will have to assert yourself. A good example of what you can expect to happen and what your response should be is as follows: Satan comes to the mind of JESUS. Satan tried to wear JESUS down. JESUS argued with him. JESUS disputed with him, but the real victory came when JESUS asserted HIS faith and said, "Get out of here devil and leave me alone." IT ISWRITTEN. (Matthew4)

And in this thing called life, you are going to have to assert yourself. There will be times you will argue, dispute and assert yourself. Stand and say," I believe GOD!" JESUS has given the dynamics of living and overcoming life to enter the CREATIVEZONE. AND I CHOOSE!!

This day l will enter the CREATIVE ZONE, and I will blame no one for my failures anymore. And I will not ever be in denial on anything again. For today, I will make CORRECT CHOICES, CORRECT DECISIONS, AND HAVE CORRECT RESULTS in my life. Because l will put forth the effort to learn the information of how to make lifework and I will overcome any and all adverse situations. For today I choose to believe the truth and allow it access in my life as I enter the CREATIVEZONE. .

PART II

IMAGINATION

CHAPTER EIGHT

IMAGINATION

M an is a unique creation. We are made in the very image of GOD. We are Spirit, Soul, Body. Three distinct parts with distinct functions of their own. But, yet these three parts make up the whole man - you. We need to know ourselves and how we were designed, and how to become operational in every area. For the word of GOD is quick and powerful and sharper than any two-edged sword, piercing even to the dividing asunder of soul and spirit, and of the joints and marrow's and is a discerner of the thoughts and intents of the heart. (Hebrew 4:12)

Dividing Asunder is a Greek word MERISMOS which is made from two other Greek root words: Merizo, which means to part to apportion, to disunite, to separate. Meros, which means to get as a section or allotment, a division or share. Merisos means a separation or distinction made between separate parts.

The WORD OF GOD separates the soul and spirit of a man. That is the only thing that can, "THE WORD." We need to know ourselves. We need to understand the separate parts and their functions.

The first division of mans is of the Soul. The soul is made up of the mind, will, emotions, and intellect. Now, that is not all the possible separations. The Dividing Asunder means to take the myriad facets of your life, break them down and clarify them. Each of the three main divisions of the SOUL can be divided into five categories.

1) THE MIND- Can be divided into the areas of imagination, reasoning, thought, logic, and intellect. The all can be summed up in one word - understanding. The soul of a man desires to possess knowledge. He uses the above stated functions to accumulate information for the purpose of coming to a conclusion, the putting together of 2+2. 2)

2) THE WILL – The will is made up of decision, choice, intent, purpose and desire. These five things can be summed up as determination.

3) EMOTIONS - The emotions are made up of the five physical senses; sight, taste, touch, smell and hearing. In this area there are other things such as hatred, love and so forth. These can be summed up as feelings. We are going to look at how to take the INVISIBLE AND BRING IT INTO THE VISIBLE, the spirit into the physical. While we look not at the things which are seen, but at the things which are NOT SEEN. For the things which are seen are temporal. But the things which are not seen are eternal. (II Corinthians4:18) In other words, the things which are temporal or temporary are SUBJECT TO CHANGE. Anything you can see, or your senses can contact are MOLDAB LE, CHANGEABLE, and REMOVABLE. BUT he goes on to say the things which are NOT what they seem are eternal and they are NOT subject to change. Now, Faith is the assurance of things hoped for, the CONVICTION or E.VIDENC E of things not seen. By faith, we understand that the worlds were framed - by the WORD OF GOD... So that what is seen was not made from things which are visible. (Hebrew s 11:1-3) Here we are again, the INVISIBLE REALM. Framed is the word, MOLDED. If you framed a house, you know what the house would look like ... And the framing of the world was through the WORD OF GOD. It was framed by the WORD OF GOD.

4) The WORD OF GOD is our authority and the basis for our faith. GOD WATCHES OVER HIS WORD TO PERFORM IT AND

CONFIRM IT. WE ARE GOING TO LEARN HOW TO RENEW OUR MINDS, BRING OUR MINDS IN HARMONY WITH OUR SPIRITS... SEE, THE MIND IS PART OF THE SOUL. You are a spirit. You do not have a spirit; you are a spirit. You have a soul, which is your mind, will, emotions and intellect. I's extremely hard for many people to believe the Spirit World is real because they cannot see it. So, to them it does not exist, because they cannot see it, touch it... But the Scriptures tell us the Spirit World is 'THE REAL WORLD." Whatever you can see, or touch is temporal and is subject to change, but the Spirit World is permanent and it is NOT subject to change. But this world and things in it that we can use our five senses to contact is only temporary and is subject to change. But how? The Word of GOD gives us the basis for our faith.

5) FAITH IS A SUBSTANCE. Faith demands action. HE'S telling us that THE MIND, the THINKING, THE THOUGHT REALM, THROUGH THE VEHICLE OF THE MIND. (The mind has two sides.) The logical, analytical reasoning side, which is the LOGOSMOS. The other side, the creative side, ANOIA-\, is the imagination. DIA simply means THROUGH...THROUGH YOUR LOGIC, which in Greek DIALOGOSMOS, or THROUGH YOUR IMAGINATION. DIANOIA is Greek. Imagination - The faculty of making mental images and things NOT PRESENT. Imagine - Picture to oneself. Man is a unique creation made in the image of GOD. let us compare.

Angels and demons operate only in the spirit realm. Animals operate in purely physical realm. But man can contact both realms. Man can operate in BOTH REALMS, the physical and the spiritual. We are an exciting and unique creation, created in the very image of GOD. We are Spirit, Soul and Body.

The Soul is the PENDULUM of the Spirit.

It screams to contact the physical realm FROM INVISIBLE TO VISIBLE. It is our logical mind that we contact the mental realm or physical realm.

And then as we swing over to the DIANOIA., THE IMAGINATION, it's our soul that contacts THE REALM OFTHE SPIRIT.

For example, teachers are analytical and logical. They reason and put it together in an understandable fashion. But if a person is highly developed. in that area alone, the ANALYTICAL and LOGIC, and do not understand how to move in the spirit, that's hopeless.

Now, the other side of the coin. People from Asian countries are highly developed in the spirit. They talk with angels, see visions, and are very aware of things. But if they have NO SUBSTANCE, NO WORD, well, they can get off in error. And you are in an extremely dangerous place because the enemy will lead you if you only have the realm of the spirit. You are easily lead if you do not have a foundation of the Word of GOD. YOU NEED BOTH!

The greatest lack I find in America is in the area of the DIANOIA, the imagination. We have the WORD, the foundation. But we do not KNOW HOW TO MOVE OUT OF THAT AND MOVE INTO THE SPIRIT AND BACK AGAIN. We must learn the principles and process.

Man is a unique creation designed to operate in both the Spirit World and Physical World. The SOUL IS THE PENDULUM, that swings between the two. And in the soul realm, the imagination is powerful. GOO deals with us based on our DIANOIA, "THROUGH OUR IMAGINATION." To GOD, it's a reality!

Jesus said, "love the lord your GOD with all your heart and soul and then HE said with all our mind. Okay. They MIND is part of the soul. So why repeat yourself? He says to love the lord with all your heart and soul and then he comes <u>down to a specific</u>. HE SAVS MIND!!

But the soul is made up of the MIND, WILL and EMOTIONS. The word MIND here translates to DIANOIA, THE IMAGINATION, the creative side of your mind.

This is not a mere suggestion, but a command that we need to bring our DIANOIA, imagination in subjection to the Word of GOO. We are to renew our minds to the Word of GOO so we can be changed, transformed. Satan is a master at programming your imagination. He has had a lot of practice! It's time we begin to operate in the proper manner or fashion as GOD designed us.

And GOD does NOT deal with us through the logical, analytical side, but GOD DEALS WITH US THROUGH OUR DIANOIA, OUR IMAGINATION. Imagination-The faculty of making mental images of things not present. Pictures to oneself. Jesus said in scriptures, 'If a man looks upon a woman with LUST, he is guilty of adultery." (Matthew 5:28) He did not say he's going to be, he said HE WAS.

Where do you lust? In your imagination. Images. You do not see words, you see images. Images are created by thoughts. Jesus said if that's the case, then you are judged guilty already. You do not have to do it, because if you CONCEIVED THAT IMAGE in the spirit, YOU ARE GUILTY OF IT!

Let me tell you why. Because once it is conceived.in the spirit, the very next thing you will do is act it out in the flesh or in your life. That is where premeditated murder comes. You picture it, you plan it, you do it!! IMAGES, IMAGINATION. NOTE: Thoughts are outside your mind. The enemy will fire firey darts of thoughts at your mind. You will always have the choice to accept and think those thoughts or reject those thoughts.

Remember, whether the thoughts are good or bad, as you accept and continually think those thoughts, repeatedly something happens! Those thoughts go from your mind down to your spirit and from your spirit into your heart. The heart it refers to is the core of the real you, where you soul and all its facets and your spirit meet. When it gets to that place, those thoughts you have allowed to be conceived, will begin to come out and produce the results or fruit of those thoughts.

They will either be GOOD or BAD results. Thinking the thought is not wrong but accepting It or allowing it to get a stronghold in your mind, to conceive is wrong if it's an evil/ bad thought. If your heart condemns you, you are already condemned. When that bad or evil thought comes you are not wicked just because you thought something, because you can do something about that!! You can reject that thought and refute it. You can say this is not my thought and I do not receive it; this thought does not come from GOD nor resonate with my spirit. GET OUT!!

You have that choice. It will all boil down to what kind thoughts you put in your mind. For your thoughts will dictate your IMAGINATION.

Joel 2: 27-28 a major prophecy, says in the last days, when the Holy Spirit is poured out, YOUR YOUNG MEN SHALL SEE VISIONS. In other words, they are going to look to the future, AND YOUR OLD MEN WILL DREAM DREAMS. (They will look back to the past. But the point is, THEY BOTH TRANSLATE BACK TO PICTURES...IMAGES. And the language the spirit realm is not words, but It is "IMAGES, DREAMS, VISIONS.

In studying the Old and New Testaments, you will find in many cases when GOD spoke to men, he would speak in dreams and visions, through an image. The heart of a man is the canvass of the Lord and the Holy Spirit is the artist. The Holy Spirit twill take the oil and use the pen, which is the tongue, and will begin to paint an image on the canvass of your heart.

As GOD shows you. But the enemy knows how to do that as well. To GOD, our imagination, DIANOIA, is not an eerie, spooky thing. To HIM, it's a reality and he deals with us through it. We think in images. WE THINK

IN IMAGES. WE DREAM IN IMAGES AND ONCE THAT IMAGE IS CONCEIVED IN THE SPIRIT, IT WILL MANIFEST IN THE FLESH OF OUR LIFE. If you can conceive it and believe it, and stay focused with it long enough, YOU'LL HAVE IT. "But I say to you that everyone who looks on a woman to lust for her has committed adultery with her already in her heart." {Matthew 5:28)

HAS COMMITTED IS PAST TENSE. Where did he commit adultery? In his heart. Please note in scriptures that when HEART is used in context with thinking it is always DIANOIA, "THE IMAGINATION OF THE HEART." Unforgiveness is exactly, the same thing. Every time you see a person, up comes the image, or thought of what they did to you. It is a picture. And all those emotions come up again. UNFORGIVENESS. The DIA\-LOGASMOS (through logic) The logical side, the teaching, contacts the physical realm, the mental realm. The Dianoia (through imagination) contacts the spirit realm and is the key to moving and operating in the spirit. ITS THE GATEWAY. Way back in the book of Beginnings for mankind, in the BOOK OF GENESIS, a story is told about some men who were not Godly.

You could call them unbelievers. The story says GOD comes down to check on them. Now, the whole earth had ONE Language and ONE SPEECH. And as it came to pass, as mankind journeyed from the east, they found a plain in the land of Shinar, so they dwelt there. These men were unified in all that they did or spoke. They said to one another, "Come let us make bricks and bake them thoroughly." They had bricks for stone, and they had asphalt for mortar. They were all in agreement and spoke. "Come let us build ourselves a city and a tower whose top is in the heavens. (There is more exciting information on this subject in my book - PYRAMID POWER.)

Let us make a name for ourselves lest we be scattered abroad over the face of the whole earth. But the Lord GOD came down to see the city and the tower which the sons of man had built. And the Lord said, "INDEED THE PEOPLE ARE ONE AND THEY ALL HAVE ONE LANGUAGE AND THIS IS WHAT THEY BEGIN TO DO NOW. Nothing that they propose or IMAGINED doing will be withheld from them. (Genesis 11:1-6) The Lord GOD is the creator of man. He knew how HE designed us to operate. He Saw that they had already built something into their hearts. They are all seeing and saying the same thing. Because of that, the Lord GOD said nothing will be impossible to them.

Can you IMAGINE if we could learn to operate the way we were designed and translate this principle into all areas of our life; church, home relationships, business, on and on. If we could start to SEE THE SAME THING AND SAY THE SAME THING, THAT IS POWERFUL!!

He says nothing will be withheld, restrained from them that they imagined doing. Here in the Old Testament, there is a Hebrew word equivalent for the Greek word DIA\NOIA\ for imagination.

IT IS YET-SIR, (IMAGINATION.) I believe and teach that the key to the spirit or the key to the heart is the IMAGINATION. A key unlocks and opens. A key give access. He gives us a key. He says nothing would be impossible to anything they had imagined. IMAGINATION IS POWERFUL!!!

When studying the WORD OF GOD, you will begin to see SOME PATTERN S EMERGE. Jesus said, "Unless you come as a little child, you will NOT enter the Kingdom of Heaven." Little children have NO PROBLEM USING THEIR IMAGINATION. But as we grow older... many of us, what happens is our imagination is pushed down, repressed, neglected to the place, in many cases, The only active side of your DLA. NOIA (imagination) is on the negative. We continually think and meditate on fear, worry and anxiety.

And for the most part, we are really good at it. We go to bed PICTURING things that we DO NOT want to happen to us. That is what fills our thought process, FEAR AND ANXIETY. And the Bible calls it a SIN. Anything that will separate you from GOD, is a sin. FEAR IS INDIRECT OPPOSITION TO FAITH. And WITHOUT FAITH, it is IMPOSSIBLE TO PLEASE GOD. Fear will also kill you quicker than most things. Fear is destructive. Fear is deadly.

We need to RETRAIN and RENEW some things in the spirit. We are made in the image and likeness of GOD. GOD uses this same principle. GOD conceived an image into HIS heart. Then HE SPOKE it out and released it. He said, "Let there be light." And there was tight. There was an IMAGE on the inside of HIM. Please understand, words are conveyors of images. There is an IMAGE inside of GOD. He framed it into words and released it into the physical realm, from invisible to visible. Some of the principles that we are to use: There's an IMAGE inside of you. Frame it into words and release it into the physical realm. "THE HEART IS THE CONNECTION." Believe or doubt in your heart! THAT'S THE SPIRITUAL CONNECTION. THE PHYSICAL RELEASE IS WHEN YOU SPEAK IT OUT OF YOUR MOUTH.

But first thing is first. First it is a thought, then it must be CONCEIVED. Sometime, because of the CONSTANT INFLUENCES in our life in the negative, it may take some time for you to change that picture or image you have on the inside. We have looked at Abraham, the Jewish patriarch, who was considered. GOD'S friend and the Father of the Faith.

It took some twenty-four years for him to Conceive AN IMAGE IN HIS SPIRIT, and it took him three months to confess it. He and his wife, Sarah, were pregnant at one hundred years of age. It took some time to change that image or picture of NO CHILDREN, BEING BARREN into an image of a Promised Son.

But he changed by the WORD OF GOD and had a son. And you can change too! YOU CAN RE-PROGRAM YOURSELF TO CREATE IN THE CREATIVE ZONE1 When GOD created man, HE said, "let us create man in our image." MAN IS CREATED IN THE IMAGE OF GOD. Now, we cannot be physically like GOD. So spiritually we are created in GOD'S own image. Now, if we are created in GOD'S image, we also operate the same way. GOD formed, first, MAN'S BODY in the dust of the earth. Then he breathed into man, the spirit. BUT WHAT HAPPENED ABOUT THE SOUL? When the BODY AND THE SPIRIT UNITED, the soul was created.

That is the contact between the two, body and spirit. It's the soul. THE SOUL IS THE PENDULU M THAT SWINGS OR CONTACTS THE PHYSICAL REALM AND THE SPIRIT REALM. "THE SOUL IS THE CONTACT AREA." The battle for life is in this realm. The enemy is NOT going to do anything about your spirit for if you are born again, you receive an instantaneous birth in the spirit of man and that is where GOD dwells, where the Holy Spirit dwells. And the enemy does not even have to do anything with your body, because all he has to do is CONTROL YOUR SOUL REALM; your mind, will, and emotions, THOUGHTS and it will manifest in your body anyway. Remember in the first chapter we looked at a word called Psychosomatic. PSYCHO, THE MIND, IS ATTEMPTING TO MANIFEST ITSELF OVER SOMA, THE BODY. ARTHRITIS IS A PRIME EXAMPLE. Unforgiveness, rigid, unbending mental patterns manifest this way in the flesh.

The Spirit-man the whole man is what is created in the image of GOD. And when the spirit and body meet, you have a "LIVING SOUL," which is the pendulum between the two. God deals with us through our DIANOIA, or our CREATIVE IMAGINATION SIDE. Most Christians that say they hear form GOD, do not. They are listening to their own soulish realm. And there is a big difference in listening to the voice of THE SPIRIT and listening to your own SOULISH REALM. See, Satan knows how to effectively program your Soulish Realm. He knows how to influence you. AND WE NEED TO LEARN HOW TO DIFFERENTIATE BETWEEN THE TWO. ITS THE WORD OF GOD that will differentiate the voice of your soul, the voice of the spirit and the voice of the HOLY SPIRIT. It's only the WORD OF GOD that WILL BUILD US UP TO A PLACE WHERE WE CAN START TO TUNE OUR EARS AND HEAR.

We must RENEW our minds daily to the WORD OF GOD so we can be transformed or effect change. The WORD OF GOD is powerful and quick. The WORD OF GOD can divide, separate, and bring total understanding to life. But you must allow that. YOU CHOOSE!! You are to, therefore, lay aside all filthiness and overflow of wickedness and RECEIVE with meekness the implanted engrafted word which is able to

SAVE YOUR SOULS. (James 1:21) You must allow THE ENGRAFTED AND IMPLANTED WORD OF GOD, which has the power and ability to save your souls. When we talk about becoming born again in your spirit, at that point Jesus Christ enters in your life and you are made NEW, PERFECT, WHOLE AND COMPLETE. However, your soul; mind, will and emotions, goes unsaved, unrenewed. The way you obtain salvation for your souls, our Soulish Realm, is the ENGRAFTED WORD OF GOD. That is what will save your souls. Engrafted means: embedded, in a fixed place, engrafted in your soul. The WORD OF GOD must become embedded in your VERY CHARACTER, PERSONALITY AND NATURE in the society in which we live, we are all programmed for QUICK FIX for everything. That's our MODERN SOCIETY MENTALITY. Especially in church. People will come in to perhaps get delivered from a STRONGHOLD in their life. They want relief and want it now. They think the church is Burger King. They won't it now and their way. But they've NOT allowed THE WORD OF GOD to become engrafted in their souls yet. And they really don't want to put any effort into the WORD OF GOD. They just want it automatically to happen. They want a spiritual OSMOSIS.

They'll exclaim, I tried GOD. I tried HIS WORD. It does not work. And they become frustrated and angry at GOD. In reality they say THE WORD a couple of times. NO MAGIC HAPPENS, so they give up! So, with Misplaced ANGER at GOD, they live on with their STRONGHOLD or problem, but now they've added ANGER and soon bitterness will Follow on and on.

For example, Women in particular who are highly motivated. The reason these women have so much trouble with alcohol or legalized narcotics or even being overweight is BECAUSE THEY WANT A QUICK FIX!! THEY ARE USED TO DOING AND SEEING RESULTS. But you must become disciplined and allow THE WORD to become ENGRAFTED in you. Allow the renewing of your mind to the WORD OF GOD and change will follow.

NOTE: PRAYER WORKS THE WONDERS OF GOD! PRAYER CHANGES THINGS. BUT PLEASE UNDERSTAND, YOU CAN BE PRAYED FOR, HAVE HANDS LAID ON YOU, AND YOU CAN FEEL ONE HUNDRED PERCENT BETTER, BUT YOU WANT YOUR VICTORY AS A LIFESTYLE. THEN YOU ARE RESPONSIBLE TO DO SOMETHING. YOU MUST DISCIPLINE YOURSELF DAILY GOING ABOUT THE TASK OF EMBEDDING THE WORD OF GOD INTO YOUR SOUL; MIND WILL AND EMOTIONS. THIS MUST TAKE PLACE FOR OUR SOULS TO LINE UP WITH OUR SPIRITS AND SPIRIT OF GOD.

I call that a SPIRITUAL EQUINOX, total alignment of spirit, soul, and body to the WORD OF GOD. If you can get to the place, you SEE IT, SAY IT, AGREE WITH IT, YOU CAN HAVE IT, the true spirit, soul and body. (Equinox) Sometimes, we as Christians stay in denial of what is really going on in our lives. We feel by ignoring the facts, they will just go away. But that is NOT true. We must learn to look at everything in our lives HONESTLY. Assess it and then with the HIGHEST TRUTH, THE HIGHEST AUTHORITY OF ALL, bring that fact in line with GOD'S WORD.

Before I continue with Imagination, I feel it pertinent to make a detour and give you, my friends, information that will help you get OUT OF Any SITUATION YOU ARE IN. IF YOU WILL, HEAR THESE WORDS FROM GOD AND ALLOW THEM TO BECOME Engrafted OR EMBEDDED IN YOU. YOU WILL BE CHANGED!!! CREATIVE ZONE,

CHAPTER NINE

HOW TO GET OUT OF ANYTHING

Now, to begin. We will take our premise from (Jonah II). GOD, the creator has given us a great plan for our life to work, but sometimes we mess up pretty bad and land in situations where we don't know what to do. So did Jonah. Jonah was a great prophet of GOD in the Old Testament. Jonah had some REAL information that got him set free and we need to know what that information is. Because if we can LEARN and use the same principles that got Jonah out of the belly of the whale, well honey, you can get out of anything. (It all depends on you allowing the WORD OF GOD to be engrafted in you.)

If Jonah had laid down in the belly of that big old fish and complained and blamed GOD, been mad, angry and bitter with GOD and everyone else, you and I would never have heard his story, because he could have never written it. He would have been digested! Now, the Lord had prepared a great fish to swallow Jonah and Jonah was in the belly of the fish for three days and three nights. Then Jonah prayed to the Lord, his GOD and said: "I cried out to the Lord because of my affliction, and he answered me. Out of the belly of Sheol (death) I cried, and you heard me. You heard my voice!

Or you cast me into the deep into the heart of the sea., and the floods surrounded me; all your billows and your waves passed over me. Then I said, 'I have been cast out of your sight.' Yet, I will look again toward your holy temple. The waters surround me, even to my soul. The deep closed around me; weeds were wrapped around my head. With its bars closed behind me forever. Yet, YOU have brought me up, my life from the pit, O Lord, my GOD. When my SOUL FAINTED within me, I remembered the Lord. And my prayer, my communication went up to YOU, into your holy temple. Those who regard worthless idols, LYING VANITIES, forsake their own mercy. But I will sacrifice to you with the voice of Thanksgiving. I will pay what I have vowed." Salvation is of the Lord. So, the Lord spoke to the fish and it vomited Jonah on dry land. (Jonah, Chapter II)

Our Goal is to walk in the spirit, allow the SPIRIT OF GOD to override through our spirits to the Soulish Realm. For the SPIRIT OF GOD giveth life!

We are SPIRIT, SOUL, AND BODY. Each has their function, but all parts of the (1) man. All these parts with their components make up man. Each are especially important. your body or flesh is just vehicle or house for your spirit and soul. Flesh is just a vehicle, but a particularly important part of you. It is kind of like this story. A little boy was asked by his science teacher to describe the flesh on his body. He answered, "It's a cover to keep people who look at you from THROWING UP!"

Well, that's a GOOD EXPLANATION. Far too many people try and emphasize just the spirit part of a man, thus bringing on imbalance. They denigrate the soul and body parts. They feel if they can somehow abuse themselves, suffer or whatever, that they will be made better for it. Putting down flesh(body) and talking bad about your Soulish Realm (mind, will, emotions, imagination and intellect) · is NOT where it is! Jesus never invited us to do that!! Each part of the whole man has its own job or function to perform. All three parts are designed good. Your flesh Is just a vehicle. Flesh was NOT designed to be a GOD.

Flesh does not make a good God. See, if you take something out of its purpose and attempt to apply it to something else and then it cannot line up with what you were trying to get it to - that it was not designed for in the first place, then it's not the thing's fault! For example, it would be like getting out on the racetrack on a jackass in the Kentucky Derby and shooting him between the eyes because he cannot win. He was not bred for that. It is not fair to him.

The horses that run in the horse races are especially bred for that. So, by you putting YOUR FLESH (body) in the position to do something it's NOT BUILT to do and then beating yourself up because you aren't accomplishing that is a little bit silly. Don't you agree! You must get it in proper perspective. FLESH IS JUST A VEHICLE. And you should love your flesh, love your body. Your flesh is good. GOD chose it as a vessel to veil, you spirit and soul. I KNOW YOU KNOW THAT YOU ARE A TEMPLE OF THE HOLY SPIRIT. So, take care of it. Watch your diet. Exercise. Be clean. Look good. Take good care of yourself and let the health of GOD be there!!

Okay. The soul realm: mind, will, emotions and intellect, is not your source of strength either. It is not built to be. The soulish realm is not bad. Take care of your mind. Have good mental hygiene. Think good and positive thoughts! The reason some can't make that work is because they try and use 'WILLPOWER ALONE" That is good when it is RENEWED BY THE WORD OF GOD to get in your spirit, but alone it will not work. For it is out of your spirit that Life come.

Revelation has to come from the spirit. BUT it is translated and becomes a part of your intellect, part of your mind working totally together. This transfer is what Apostle Paul was talking about when he said, 0 Let this mind be in you, which is Christ Jesus. How are you going to get this information that comes to your spirit transferred over to the checking account of your soul?

It must be transferred before it can be spent. It becomes a part of your LIFE, becomes a Revelation, and has to become a part of your thought life. Then you read it. As a man thinketh in his heart, so is he. So, he does. (Proverbs) That's why you must decide to live according to the principles of GOD'S WORD and learn to walk in the spirit. You do not have to be so religious and feel you have to Stop every thirty minutes and have a prayer meeting over every decision you make. YOU CAN WALK IN THE WILL OF GOD. The reason so, is because you have transferred from spirit to soul. Different functions -But THE SOURCE IS "THE SPIRIT." You must learn to FEED YOUR SPIRIT-MAN. Your SPIRIT-MAN does not eat movies and junk. It might be entertaining, and you enjoy it.

That is okay, but let it be in moderation, because your spirit-man is not going to be fed. As a matter of fact, you can starve your spirit-man to death eating that kind of stuff only. I believe where it says, "If any man defiles the spirit, GOD will destroy him." I think we can defile our spirit. Defile is a synonym for destroy. So how do you destroy the spirit? You STARVE IT TO DEATH. You could starve your flesh and commit suicide one day at a time by starving. People do it all the time. It is the same way you destroy your spirit-man. You starve it to death. Your spirit-man DOES NOT eat movies, steak, potatoes, hobbies, going out on the to.vn, sports, or vacations to Jamaica.

All those are good for what they were designed and intended, but they will NOT feed your spirit. Your spirit that is trapped within you (if you will) CAN BE STARVED TO DEATH. So, we are the whole man, spirit, soul and body. Let us understand the functions. Through the realm of the spirit comes revelation, strength, and power. Then we must get it somehow transferred over to the Soul Realm. (mind will and emotions)

The spirit-man a born-again believer is the headquarters where GOD DWELLS.

Now let us truly make life work, by living as Jesus taught us,

SEEK FIRST THE KINGDOM OF GOD AND ALL HIS RIGHTEOUSNESS AND ALL THESE THINGS WILL BE ADDED TO YOU. IN OTHER WORDS, LISTEN AND LEARN HOW TO OPERATE IN THE KINGDOM OF GOD.

May the Lord bless each and every one who has taken time to read and live by the instructions broken down in terms you can understand and live by. Abundantly living in God's Creative Zone.

THE END

You can contact Lady Janice through
LADY JANICE @ HALLELUJAHLADY195@GMAIL.COM

Printed in the United States
by Baker & Taylor Publisher Services